Back to Beadin'

Elegant Amulet Purses & Jewelry
Using Delica & Seed Beads

Written & Illustrated by

Barbara E. Elbe

 B.E.E. Publishing, Redding, California

First Edition: Published By B.E.E. Publishing, September 1996

Color separation by Redding Printing
1130 Continental Street
Redding, California
(916) 243-0525 Fax (916) 243-0427

Elbe, Barbara E., 1945-
    Back To Beadin' /by Barbara E. Elbe

    ISBN   0-9653622-1-3

Library of Congress Catalog Number: 96-86177

Acknowledgments

Most of all I want to thank my husband, Larry. I spent countless hours, 7 days a week working on the computer and beading designs, not much company. When I wasn't working on the book, I was talking about it. He was always willing to listen and to encourage me to keep going when I got discouraged.

Additionally, I want to thank a very good friend, Vickie Lamoureux, who had the talent to find my typographical and grammatical errors, no matter how small they were.

I also want to thank a very nice person, Lowell Martinson, for the outstanding photography work.

Table of Contents

Table of Contents

Select Bibliography

Blakelock, Virginia. "*Those Bad, Bad Beads*," Walsonville, Oregon, 1990

Chatt, David. "*Beaded Amulet Purses*" by Nicolette Stessin, Seattle, Washington
    Beadworld Publishing, 1994

Kliot, Jules & Kaethe. "*Bead Work*," Berkeley, California 94703
    Lacis Publications, Revised Ed., 1991

Introduction

Unlike my first two books, **Beaded Images** and **Beaded Images II**, that dealt with just earrings, this book expands into other areas of beading and introduces a few new weaving techniques. Exploring and learning new ideas is so important in keeping one's interest.

I find amulet purses the most fun because they are like little paintings, the pictures' capabilities can be endless. There are 10 patterns included in this book ranging from a variety of birds in picturesque scenes, a classic Persian cat, to a bouquet of flowers in a vase with a few petals falling off. Also, there is the herringbone purse which is quite beautiful. Even though it is all done in one color, the weave gives it a very unique look. The last one is a tiny purse done in right angle weave. The strap is also done in the same weave with a clasp added.

There is a complete chapter giving detailed instructions on how to achieve the different weaves. Most of the purses are done in brick stitch, not peyote stitch. How to construct the horizontal purses in a tube fashion, and how to sew together the vertical purse will be explained.

I used to crochet before getting hooked on beading. I found instructions on how to crochet beaded cord necklaces out of an old book from the turn-of-the-century. This was perfect for me, as it combined my two loves, beading and crocheting. Instructions are included on how to make these beautiful pieces of jewelry. The work, when completed, is so flexible it can be tied into a knot. People have asked me if they are peyote stitch, but peyote is very stiff. These pieces can be made with either Delica or seed beads. Done out of the Delica they glisten beautifully and look very expensive. If you know how to crochet, you have to try these. They are a little hard to get started, but once you get the idea, they go fast.

There is a short chapter on how to make daisy chain bracelets and necklaces. These are so pretty and easy to make. Seed beads are the best choice for these. The double daisy chain bracelet is a little more difficult. I have given instructions on making them with either Delica or seed beads.

There are just a few earring designs in this book. The hummingbird started out as an earring, then it was made into a purse with flowers added. This makes a beautiful set. The bouquet earrings were made to go with the bouquet purses.

The ornament idea came up around Christmas time. The Christmas earrings and Santa pin from **Beaded Images** work perfect. I have included instructions on how put together one of these ornaments with the year-round perfect choice, the hummingbird.

All of the patterns in this book are graded for difficulty, * easiest to ***** most difficult. What makes some of the purses more difficult is their uniqueness-- i.e., stick or even fringe, rounded top and bottom, strap or type of weave.

I hope you enjoy this book as much as I enjoyed putting it together and that it will be an inspiration for you to try new ideas. I don't believe everything that can be made from beads has been discovered yet. Many new ideas are still hidden within us.

Beading Supplies

Having the right beading supplies and tools is very important. When first getting started, a visit to a store specializing in beads would be a good idea. There they can help you make the right selections, answer your questions and give you a good start. This is important. Regular craft stores are limited for supplies and good advice.

Beads Of course the most important ingredient in beading is the bead. First you have to decide what type and size of bead for the project. In this book, Delica and seed beads are used. My first love is Delica; although, I originally started out with seed.

Delica/Antique These are fairly new to the United States. Delica (DB) are imported from Japan where they are produced by Miyuki Shoji Co., Ltd. There is also another brand called Antique by Toho. They are very much alike and come in many similar colors. Last count, DB had approximately 400 colors to choose from. What I like best is their consistency in size and their very large holes, quite unlike seed beads. They are a little smaller than 11/o seed beads, more the size of 12/o but taller. I have also heard them called Japanese cylinder beads, probably because of their shape. Although I would love to use DB in everything I make, they are not suited for everything because of their shape. In some designs, like the daisy chain, round works better. So don't throw away your seed beads, they are still very useful.

DB can be bought either in 5 to 10 gram packages, or 4 to 8 gram tubes. Wholesale places sell in bulk, 100 gram to kilo packs. These beads are expensive but worth it.

Hexagon Another cylinder shaped bead, smaller than DB with thinner walls. They are about the size of the 14/o seed bead but, again, taller. Although they are fairly consistent, they are not as good as DB but better than seed. Hexagon (HEX) are easier to find in stores but do not have as good a color selection. Many of them come in the hexagon shape (six sided) which gives them an extra shine.

HEX are usually sold in the same quantities as the DB, but less expensive. Some opaque colors come in hanks. These beads are a worthwhile addition; although not used in this book. They are very lightweight and work especially well for larger earrings.

Seed The old faithful, been around forever, bead. They come in a variety of sizes: 9/o, largest to 16/o, smallest. There are smaller seed beads, 18/o to 22/o, but these are hard to find and if acquired, they are so tiny a magnifying light is needed to work with them. Colors also become more limited in the smaller beads. The most popular size and available in an almost unlimited variety of colors is 11/o. I have used these in a few of the purses, the daisy chain bracelets and necklaces.

Seed beads usually come in hanks but are sometimes sold by the gram in packs or tubes. They are the least expensive of the three types listed. Most seed come from Czechoslovakia. Japan is now importing some very nice colors with larger holes.

Needles It is important to buy needles that are made especially for beading. They are very thin and flexible, perfect for those tiny holes. Do not use regular sewing needles.

Beading needles come in a range of sizes, from very thin size 16, to thicker size 12. The higher the number the thinner the needle. I have been told that the size of the needle corresponds to the size of beads being used. This I am not sure of. What I have found works best is size 12 for DB, HEX and most of the 11/o seed beads. Then have a few thinner size 15 needles around for the times your size 12 won't go through the beads.

Depending on how many passes are made with the thread through a bead effects the size of the needle used. Never force a needle through. The bead can break and ruin the piece being worked. It can be annoying having to change to a thinner needle in the middle of a project, but having a bead break can be far worse.

Thread Do not use regular sewing thread. The most commonly available thread made especially for beading is Nymo®, found in black or white. It does come in colors but is hard to find. It is a strong, multi-fiber nylon thread.

√ A permanent color marking pen works well for coloring white thread. Either color the threads that show on the outer edge, or color the whole section of thread before using by running the thread over the side part of the felt tip.

There are a variety of thicknesses to choose from. They range from 000 to 0 (thin to thicker) and A, B and D. A is the thinnest of this group, B is about the same as 0 and D being thickest of all. I prefer to use 0 for most of the earrings and smaller jewelry, and D for purses, necklaces and bracelets as it adds strength and rigidity. They can be purchased in two sizes. Most easily found is the bobbin size (*Figure 8-a*) with approximately 160 yards (depending on the thickness of thread), and large 3 ounce (*Figure 8-b*) cone size, which only comes in black or white. If you do a lot of beading or loom work, the 3 oz. cone is very useful.

√ Bobbin size thread has a tendency to curl easier than spool thread. Wetting and stretching it before it is waxed will help to alleviate some of this problem.

√ Waxing the thread also helps to make it more manageable. With a cube of beeswax, run the section of thread to be used over the top between the thumb and wax.

Bobbin   *3 oz. Spool*

Figures 8-a & 8-b

Materials

Beading trays There are many different types of beading trays. I started out with a simple wooden tray purchased from a local bead store. (*Figure 9-a*) After making a few minor additions, it was perfect for my needs. It measures 6" x 18" x 1", with the beading area about 3/8" deep. The deeper the tray, the harder it is to pick up beads with the needle.

√ Since the tray was exactly 18" long, I marked the top front edge like a ruler, added numbers 1" through 18" and coated them with clear nail polish to keep them from rubbing off. This works perfect for measuring thread.

√ I cut a piece of cardboard, covered it with cloth and inserted it onto the tray to give a work area where the beads would not roll out of control.

√ I added a small container on the board for a place to dispose of unwanted beads that inevitably come in every package.

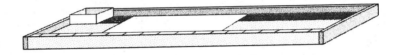

Figure 9-a

Recently I purchased a round, white porcelain watercolor dish now offered as a beading tray by some bead stores (*Figure 9-b*). It is small, measuring approximately 5 1/4" across, with 9 individual compartments to keep beads separated. A very nice plastic carrying case, approximately 8 1/2 x 12 x 2 1/2" deep, can also be purchased at an extra cost. It can hold one or two ceramic dishes, with the loose beads still in the compartments, in place by foam for storage or traveling. This is a great idea. You can take exactly what you need on a trip and have everything right there in front of you. My only problem is, because the individual compartments are small, it is difficult to get a low angle on the needle to keep the beads from sliding off when picked up. This slows my beading down considerably. I still like it, but will use it only when away from home.

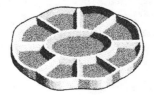

Figure 9-b

Storage Containers A variety of storage devices can be found for storing bead supplies. Plano® puts out an endless assortment of tackle boxes. Some of the larger, approximately 15" wide x 9 1/2 " deep x 15" tall, tackle boxes have an area up front where up to three large, 8 1/2 x 14", utility boxes slide in and out like drawers. These utility boxes can be divided into twenty four individual, 2 x 2", compartments for storing beads and other small items. The top of these large Plano® boxes open to another storage area for larger miscellaneous items. Plastic 2 x 2" E-Z Grip® reclosable baggies, the ones with the red stripe (they stay closed the best), or the little 2" vials work well and fit perfectly into the compartments.

Small Tools Here are some of the small tools you should have for jewelry making. (*Figure 10-a & 10-b*).

Needle Nose Pliers:	Look for the ones with smooth jaws to help prevent marking.
Round Nose Pliers:	Similar looking to needle nose pliers except the jaws are round. These are used for wrapping wire and forming loops.
Wire Cutters:	Buy good quality to prevent the tips from breaking.
Scissors:	Embroidery scissors work well because of their curved up tips. This allows for a close cut.

I purchased my better quality pliers from Sears. They cost more, but have a life-time warranty. Less expensive ones can be purchased almost anywhere.

Needle Nose   *Wire Cutters*

Figure 10-a & 10-b

Adhesives E-6000® will bond to almost anything. It is clear, waterproof, and most important, flexible. I find it a little difficult to spread, but so far it is the best adhesive I have found. Bead stores and catalogs carry it in 4 ounce tubes.

Lighting Good lighting is important. Of course the very best is natural light, by a window, on a clear day. This is not always available, especially in evenings or winter time. Any type of artificial light will reflect off the beads, altering their appearance. I use an adjustable fluorescent desk lamp, purchased from an office supply store, only when I have to. This can be adjusted for some control of the light. I bead during the daylight hours as much as possible. This prevents a lot of mistakes and headaches.

Beading Techniques

A variety of techniques have been used in the construction of the jewelry presented in this book. The earrings are done in brick stitch. Purses are of brick stitch, right-angle weave and herringbone. The bracelets and necklaces are done using cord crochet, even-count flat peyote stitch and daisy chain.

Brick Stitch

If you look at this completed stitch, the beads are arranged in a pattern resembling stacked bricks.

Row One The base row. Start by picking up two beads with the needle and sliding them to the measured point listed in the instructions for each pattern (*Figure 11-a*). The remaining thread is used for the second half of the design.

Figure 11-a

Hold the two beads in place with your thumb and forefinger, loop around with the needle and pass through the beads again in the same direction (*Figure 11-b*). Pull together, side by side (*Figure 11-c*).

Figure 11-b & 11-c

Add to the base row (*Figure 11-d*) until you have the amount of beads needed for the pattern being worked. Turn. All patterns are worked from left to right.

Figure 11-d

Second Row Add beads across the top of the first row (*Figures 12-a & 12-b*). Turn. Continue in this fashion following the pattern being worked. Without increasing or decreasing on the end of the rows (explained on pages 13 & 14), the beads will naturally taper to a point as shown (*Figure 12-d*).

Figure 12-a & 12-b

Ideally, the base row should be an odd number of beads allowing the second half of the thread to be positioned correctly for the second half of the design. Sometimes the base row is an even number (*Figure 12-c*).

Figure 12-c

Repositioning takes place after the completion of the first half (*Figure 12-d*). Then just follow the illustration below, starting with the solid arrow (*Figure 12-e*). This will get you positioned correctly for the rest of the pattern.

Figure 12-d & 12-e

Increasing & Decreasing

Knowing how to increase and decrease allows you to be as creative as you wish. This is how sculpturing is achieved. Before learning how to sculpture, I was confined to the diamond and triangle shapes.

Increasing at Beginning To increase by just one extra bead, pick up two beads instead of the usual one, attach to the same place as you would have the one (*Figure 13-a*).

Figure 13-a

To increase the row by two beads at one end, follow the instructions (*Figure 13-a.*). Start at the solid arrow (*Figure 13-b*), go back through the first bead on the row, pick up a new bead, loop around and follow the arrows back to where you started. A row can be increased by as many beads as you wish in this fashion. Just keep adding to the end before going back to where you started.

Figure 13-b

Increasing at End This can be done in a couple of ways. One is to pick up a new bead, go down through the bead on the previous row (*Figure 13-c*), then back through the new bead. If there is an end thread on the previous row (end threads are not on every row), the new bead can be attached there (*Figure 13-d*).

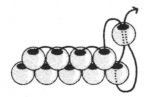

Figures 13-c & 13-d

To increase a row on the end by two or more beads, follow directions on proceeding page (*Figure 13-c or 13-d*). Then add on as shown starting at solid arrow (*Figure 14-a*).

Figure 14-a

The direction the needle ends up pointing after increasing can be very important to the continuation of the design. *Figure 14-b* shows how to change that direction. Begin at the solid arrow.

Figure 14-b

Figure 14-c is the same as *Figure 14-b* except this row is increased by three beads. On a normal increase, the needle would be facing up.

Figure 14-c

Decreasing at Beginning Just drop down to the row below and come up where the pattern being worked on shows (*Figure 14-d*). Depending how many previous rows you go down through changes how far over you will come out.

Figure 14-d

Brick Stitch For Amulet Purses

Horizontal Purse

1. Cut a section of size D Nymo® thread 5 yards long, wax.
2. Place needle just 2-3 inches in from end.

> √ Size D thread is thick making it hard to slide the needle. Having it close to the end makes it easier to take the needle on and off.
> √ The needle cuts into the thread causing it to fray. With the needle so close to the end, the damage is in an area that will not be used for the purse.
> √ Run fingers down the thread occasionally, dangling the needle and thread in the air to get the twirls in the thread out. This helps to keep the thread from tangling.
> √ It is very important when stitching the beads together to keep the tension loose. Pull the beads into place gently. This will produce an end product that is flexible. Just keep telling yourself, "relax".
> √ Re-wax the thread occasionally.

3. Pick up two beads, place 2 1/2 yards in (halfway point on thread). This allows half the thread for the upper section of the pattern, and the other half to begin lower section.
4. Create a base row with the number of beads stated in the pattern. Join ends together (*Figure 15-a*).
5. Pick up two beads following the design being worked on and attach as you would one bead (*Figure 15-b*). Continue around design.
6. Join ends together by going through the first bead at the beginning of the row and attaching to the loop of the previous row, as was done with all the other beads (*Figure 15-c*). Repeat, completing top 6-7 rows.

Figure 15-a, 15-b & 15-c

7. Add optional 2 or 3-bead lace along top row (*Figure 16-a*). To keep thread from showing in purse section, make the thread loops on inside of purse instead of outside. It is easiest to add the lace at this point

Figure 16-a

8. Attach new 2 1/2 yard sections of thread as needed, weaving end securely into purse.
9. Stitch bottom of purse together (*Figure 16-c*).

✓   I use 2 1/2 yard sections because they are easiest to handle, especially with having the needle only 2-3 inches from the end of the thread.

✓   Size D thread makes too big a knot to hide properly. Instead of a knot, I have found that just zig-zagging the thread back and forth three or four times through three or four beads each zig-zag holds it securely.

✓   Do not force the needle through too many beads at once when zig-zagging. The last thing you want is a broken bead. Size D thread is too thick to use with a needle thinner than size 12, so be very careful.

Vertical Purse

1. Cut a section of size D Nymo® thread 5 yards long, wax.
2. Place needle just 2-3 inches in from one end.
3. Pick up two beads and place 2 1/2 yards in (halfway point on thread). This will allow 2 1/2 yards of thread to start the left half of the design and another 2 1/2 yards for the beginning of the right half of the design.
4. Create the base row (usually the center row) with the number of beads stated in the pattern . <u>Do not join ends</u> <u>together</u>. Turn. Extend by one bead every other row (*Figure 16-b*). Vertical is done flat (*Figure 16-b*), bent in half when completed and joined by stitching up the sides (*Figure 16-c*).

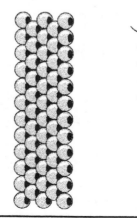

Figure 16-b & 16-c

Right Angle Weave

This technique is not as difficult as it looks, but should be practiced before starting a project. Work with a single color design the first few times to get the feel of the weave. A multi-color design is difficult to follow from the graph paper and will only be confusing. The figure eight pattern of the daisy chain is very similar. I did many daisy chains before ever trying this weave and found it helped me considerably. This technique is all done in right angle turns, clockwise and counter-clockwise, always in circles (*Figure 17-a*). Never go straight, it will cause the work to pucker (*Figure 17-b*).

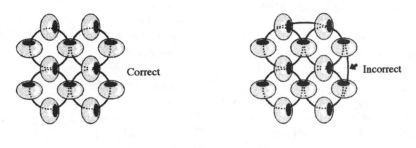

Correct   Incorrect

Figure 17-a & 17-b

Round seed beads make an even looking purse. Delica Beads also work well, but you will need more to make the same size purse. Their holes are much larger, this is a plus. Size D Nymo® thread is used for strength, but can sometimes cause difficulty with the smaller seed bead holes, especially on the third trip through the bead. It is impossible to make a purse with just one section of thread, because the circles of beads use thread rapidly. Work about 2 inches of tail back into piece going in circles to secure. Attach new sections of thread in same manner.

First Row Pick up four beads with the needle and position them approximately 6" from the end of thread. This leaves enough to tie off later. Holding the four beads between the thumb and forefinger, pass the needle back through in the same direction and pull beads into a tight circle. Tie a knot. You will notice there are two horizontal and two vertical beads (*Figure 17-c*). This is what right angle weave is made up of. Now go through the first bead after the knot to position yourself for the next loop of beads.

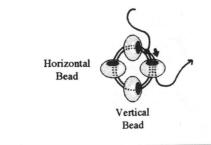

Horizontal
Bead

Vertical
Bead

Figure 17-c

Pick up three beads and go back down through that same bead in the same direction, pull tight (*Figure 18-a*). Continue as shown (*Figure 18-b*) adding three beads at a time until desired length.

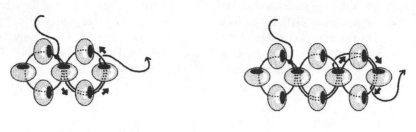

Figure 18-a & 18-b

Do not go straight up from the last bead at the end of the row to start a new row. The thread path must always go in circles, never go straight to another bead (*Figure 17-b*). These circles alternate between clockwise/counter-clockwise. Add three beads to start the new row (*Figure 18-c*). Two beads are added to complete each circle for the rest of the row (*Figure 18-d*). Use the guide provided to help view only the row being worked. Repeat until desired size. Make sure each row has the same amount of bead circles. If a circle of beads is accidently left out, the work will not lay evenly.

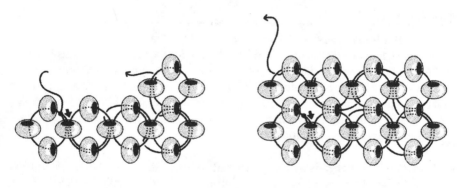

Figure 18-c & 18-d

Decreasing After adding the last two beads at the end of a row, backtrack with the thread (*Figure 18-e*) to the previous circle of beads in that same row. Begin a new row from there adding three beads, continue across row as before. Stop one circle short for an even taper on both sides.

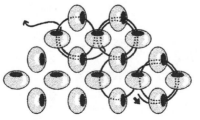

Figure 18-e

Herringbone Weave

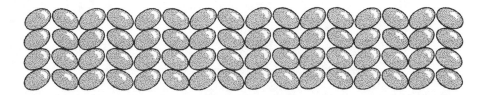

This is a unique appearing technique resembling a herringbone pattern. The weave shows up best when done in solid color. It is very different from other weaves in this book and should be practiced before starting a large project.

For this sample piece, start with a 2' section of waxed Nymo® thread, size D. Place one (stop) bead about 8" from the end leaving a tail of thread. This will be worked in later. Add the remainder of beads needed (16 total) to make up the first row of the design (*Figure 19-a*). The total of these beads must always be in multiples of 4. Now add one bead, go through #16, skip #14 & 15 beads, run needle and thread through #13 bead, add two beads, run needle through #12 bead, repeat to the end. Add two beads and go through the one shown (*Figure 19-a*), pull into place. This gives the end bead of one row and the starting bead of the next row.

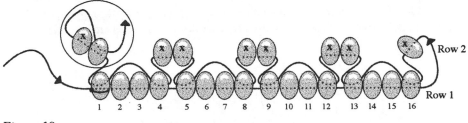

Figure 19-a

Pull everything together to form little "V's" (*Figure 19-b*). The beads with an "x" on them should be all on the top in a row when you start to pull them together. When Row 2 is added and everything is pulled together, the first row of 16 beads split and move side by side to become Row 1 and 2 of the design (*Figure 19-b*) and Row 2 becomes Row 3. Pull all the "V's" up side by side. Pull up the tension between them. Adjust them with your fingernails, causing the pairs of beads to form into the recognizable herringbone pattern. It takes practice to get an even tension in these first three rows, but it is important for the rest of the piece.

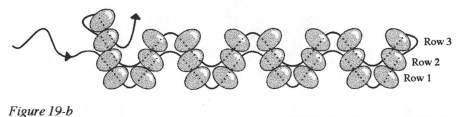

Figure 19-b

Continue with the rest of Row 4 in the same manner as Row 3 (*Figure 20-a*). This is a relatively easy weave once the first three rows are established.

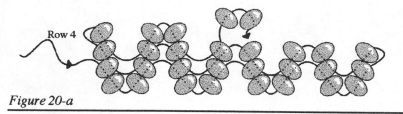

Figure 20-a

Decreasing Instead of adding two beads at end of row as explained (*Figure 19-a*), add one as shown (*Figure 20-b*), go back through bead that was just exited, up through two beads instead of one. Continue, ending one bead short on other side.

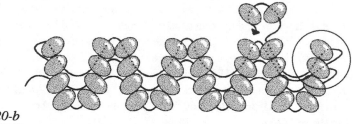

Figure 20-b

After adding last pair of that row and pulling into place, go back up through the one outer bead, add two beads and continue across (*Figure 20-c*). Repeat same at other end.

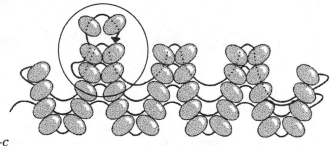

Figure 20-c

To decrease another herringbone pair, after adding last pair on row just finished and pulled into place, go back up through outer bead, down other bead (*Figure 20-d*), over to next herringbone pair and continue across, stopping one herringbone pair short on other side.

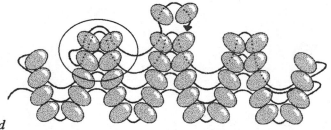

Figure 20-d

Twist & Stick Fringe
Peyote Style Strap

Twist Fringe

This is one of the prettiest fringe and it is not very difficult to do. String beads as shown (*Figure 21-a*) making sure DB beads equal same length. Even with the same count of beads, they do not always come out even because of inconsistencies. After all beads are in place, stretch strand out horizontally (*Figure 21-b*). Twist the thread between finger and thumb about three times up close to last bead. Hold these twists in place, and run the twists off other end of thread, letting needle dangle and twirl in the air. The section with misc. beads should twirl some, distributing the twists. Only the section of thread with beads on it should have twists, not the empty section of thread with the needle. Repeat this approximately 6-7 times for longer fringe, less for the shorter fringe. Still holding all the twists in place, run the needle up through the second bead over to the right along the bottom of the purse. Pull fringe into place, adjust twists. Go down the third bead over to the right with needle. Repeat across bottom of purse.

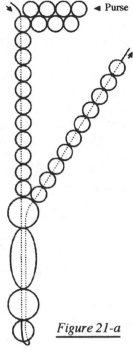

◄ Purse

Figure 21-a

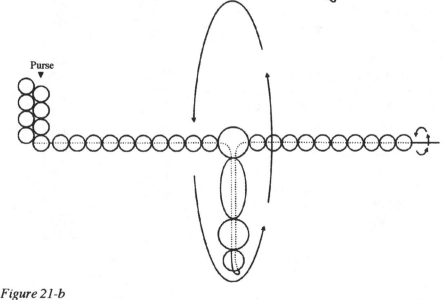

Purse

Figure 21-b

21

Stick Fringe

Stick fringe makes a very nice front or accent fringe. It is not difficult, but it does take time and a considerable amount of thread. Follow illustration (*Figure 22-a*) starting off with thirteen beads. Go around last bead, up through two. This leaves three beads for bottom branch. Add three beads, go around last one, up through the two remaining and the three on the main section. This give the first branch off the main section and puts you in position for the next branch. Repeat this to the top. The amount of beads on each branch can vary. Follow illustrations shown with each design.

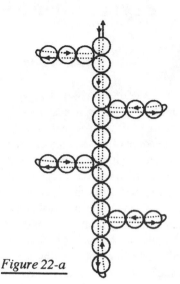

Figure 22-a

Peyote Style Strap

This strap is done with two threads attached to the front and back corner of the purse. Pick up the amount of DB beads needed for the peyote section of the strap with the first needle and thread. With the second needle and thread, pick up one DB bead, go through the next DB on the first strand, pick up another, go through next. Repeat until total needed. To achieve an even distribution of thread, slide the DB beads on the thread until they are about 1/2" from where they should be (*Figure 22-b*). Now, row by row slide them back into position (*Figure 22-c*). Do small sections at a time. If for some reason the beads have been added wrong with the second thread, you do not want to be stuck taking out a large section.

Figure 22-b & 22-c

22

Introduction To Amulet Purses

Amulet by definition is something worn on the body as a charm against evil. Amulet purses are made to carry a talisman, a magic stone or charm, for this purpose. They have also been called medicine bags. Nowadays people just wear them because they are pretty.

They are fun to make. They are like miniature canvases, giving a lot more room than an earring for creativity. I have tried a few different weaving techniques just for variety, but my favorite by far is still brick stitch. The other weaves give nice texture but are difficult for creating pictures.

Most of the purses I have seen being made these days are done in peyote stitch. The purses found in this chapter are done in brick stitch. The two stitches look the same when completed, but the techniques are completely different. I find it is easier to get the rows of beads more even and the stitch looser using brick stitch, giving the purse a soft, flexible feel. This is done by checking each bead for size before using and not pulling the thread too tight when adding the bead. Brick stitch takes a bit longer to complete, but it is worth it. Since peyote stitch is not used in any of the purse designs in this book, instructions are not included. If you prefer to use peyote stitch, there are several books to be found explaining this technique.

To me a purse without fringe is only half finished. The fringe can be as important to the design as the purse itself. It is best to wait until after the bag portion of the purse is completed before even considering what the fringe will look like. Then take the purse to a local bead store to pick out the miscellaneous beads. That way the beads are selected specifically for that purse. After the fringe is completed, the strap is done to match. So much time is used in creating the bag, why not take a little longer adding fringe to make it even better.

There are a variety of fringe. The easiest is single strands straight down from the bottom of the purse like on earrings, tapering to the middle, then back up. This is used on the Village and Star purses. There is fringe that looks like lattice work on the upper section with the fringe extending, as on the Hummingbird and Bluebird purses. But my very favorite is the twisted fringe, which has been used on all the other purses. The heaviness of the double twists gives a good balance to the bag portion. This fringe is hung from the back row of the purse leaving the front row for accent fringe.

You can follow the fringe included in each pattern or interchange them. Finding the exact miscellaneous beads used in these patterns is near impossible, but the materials list will give you an idea of what to look for and how many. Be creative, and most of all take your time. Never hurry to complete a purse. Just accept the fact that they are going to take a long time, so just bead and enjoy. In timing myself on the bouquet purse, it took approximately 22 hours for the bag portion alone, another 4 hours for the fringe and about 3 hours for the strap. This was spread over a 5 day period and did not include any of the time spent designing.

√ **Strap** There was not enough room to illustrate the whole strap clearly. Here is an example: When the instructions say to "String A, B & C", this means string A , B & C is strung from the <u>bottom</u> of the illustration up. "String B & A" in reverse means string B from the <u>top</u> of the illustration down and the same with A. Section C is not always repeated because on most purses this is the center back of the strap.

Village Purse
Brick Stitch

Materials Needed **

10 Colors of Delica & Antique
 4 2.5 mm Gold Filled
86 3 mm Gold Filled
30 6 mm Antique Gold Rosebud
 7 6x10 mm Chartreuse
13 4 mm Red Jasper
 6 8x10 mm Amethyst
 1 6x11 mm Teardrop Amethyst
    White Size D Nymo® Thread

Top Section Start 6th row down from top. Base row is 54 beads (27 front beads and 27 in back done with DB 27, Metallic Teal Iris). Work to top of pattern. Instructions for brick stitch on page 15.

Lace Add 2 beads at a time along the top edge (*Figure 16-a*) except for the center front, shown in illustration on page 26. Add the side fringe.

Side Fringe This is added at the same time as the top lace. Go down at "X" on front corner of purse, create fringe (illustrated on page 26), then up through the other "X" on back corner. Weave end of thread in securely, cut.

Bottom Section Attach the needle to the other end of thread. Continue with rest of design working in new 2 1/2 yard sections of thread as needed. Stitch bottom of purse closed (*Figure 16-c*). Weave in end, cut.

Fringe Attach 2 yard section of thread to lower left corner where shown on opposite page. Follow illustration on page 27. Weave end of threads into purse, cut.

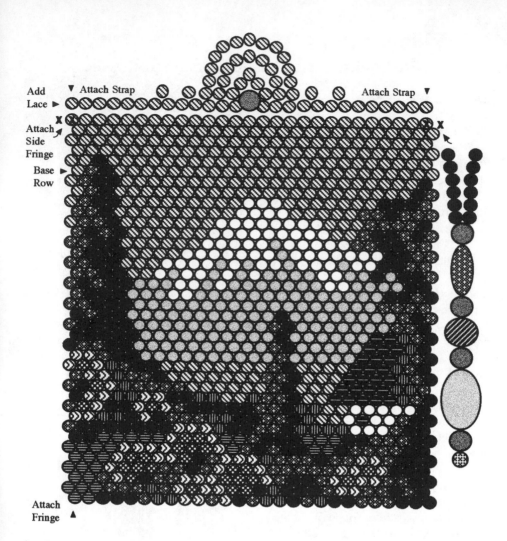

► 54 Base Row
38 Rows Long

AQ 23 S/L Light Blue		DB 201 White Pearl	
DB 27 Metallic Teal Iris		AQ 563 Galvanized Magenta	
DB 413 Galvanized Light Green		AQ 501 Metallic Copper Iris	
DB 418 Galvanized Light Rose		DB 205 Ceylon Beige	
AQ 461 Metallic Violet Iris		AQ 564 Galvanized Russet	

26

24" Strap Cut 2 sections of thread 1 yard each. Attach where shown, one thread in front corner, the other in back corner. Weave in ends at least one third way down purse, cut. Attach needles to other ends of threads. String A, B & C (150 actual beads). String B & A in reverse to finish (see page 24). Twist strap by holding double threads at end of all beads just added and flipping the purse section over and over until the desired amount of twists are obtained. Attach to the other side corner of purse while holding twists in place. Weave thread ends in same as other end, cut.

Miscellaneous Beads

8x10 mm Amethyst

6 mm Antique Gold Rosebud
3 mm Gold Filled
2.5 mm Gold filled
4 mm Red Jasper
6x10 mm Chartreuse

6x11 mm Teardrop Amethyst

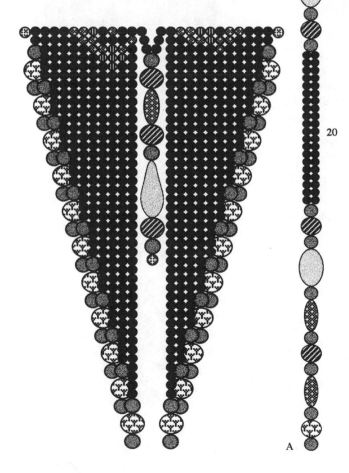

20

30

30

150

A   B   C

27

Bouquet Purse
Brick Stitch

Materials Needed *

9 Colors of Delica
9 3 mm Gold Filled
77 2.5 mm Gold Filled
15 6 mm Rose Quartz
18 6 mm Two-Tone Rose Diamond
12 7x9 mm Two-Tone Rose Oval
9 6 mm Two-Tone Rose Round
4 4 mm Clear Austrian Crystal
1 8 mm Clear Austrian Crystal
3 7 mm Antique Gold Flower
1 11x18 mm Ant. Gold Flower Teardrop
1 8x10 mm Dark Rose With Flower
   White Size D Nymo® Thread

Start 7th row down from top. Base row is 54 beads (27 front beads, and 27 in back done with DB 25, Metallic Blue Iris). See instructions for purse brick stitch, page 15. Work to top and add 2-bead lace edge (*Figure 16-a*). Weave end of thread in securely, cut.

Attach needle to other end of the thread. Continue with rest of the design working in new 2 1/2 yard sections of thread as needed. Stitch bottom of purse closed (*Figure 16-c*).

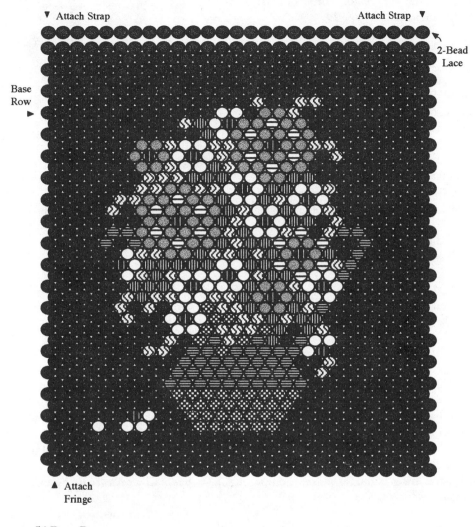

▼ Attach Strap   Attach Strap ▼

2-Bead Lace

Base Row ►

▲ Attach Fringe

► 54 Base Row
40 Rows Long

●	DB 25 Metallic Blue Iris		DB 27 Metallic Teal Iris
◉	DB 856 Matte Tr. Red Orange AB		DB 124 Trans. Chartreuse Luster
⊖	DB 70 Lined Rose Pink AB		DB 792 Dyed Matte Op. Blue Grey
○	DB 201 White Pearl		DB 859 Matte Trans. Emerald AB
◑	DB 681 Semi-Matte S/L Squash		

Front Fringe Attach 1 1/2 yard section of thread to the front bottom corner of purse where indicated on page 29.

1. Pick up 5 DB 25 (Metallic Blue Iris) beads, add misc. beads, go back through misc. beads, add 5 more Blue Iris. Go up through 5th bead over along bottom of purse, out 3rd bead making sure thread is in front of last loop.

2. Pick up 9 Blue Iris, add misc. beads, go back through misc. beads, add 9 more Blue Iris. Go up through 9th bead over, out 7th. Make sure thread is in front of last loop.

3. Add 11 Blue Iris, misc., 11 Blue Iris. Up 13th, out 11th, thread in front of last loop.

4. Add 7 Blue Iris, misc., 7 Blue Iris. Up 17th out 15th. From this time on the thread will be <u>behind</u> the previous loop.

5. 11 blue, misc., 9 blue. Up 21, out 19.

6. 9 blue, misc., 9 blue. Up 25, out 23.

7. 5 blue, misc., 5 blue. Up 27. Weave in thread, cut.

Back Fringe Attach 3 yards of thread to the back lower corner of purse. Follow illustration on page 31.

Pick up 25 DB 25 (Metallic Blue Iris), add misc. beads, go back through misc. beads, add 25 Blue Iris. Twist (see page 21).

Pay attention to where the center fringe is connected to purse. Weave in end of thread, cut.

24 " Strap Cut 2 sections of thread 1 yard each. Attach where shown, one thread in front corner and one in back. Weave ends in one third way down purse, cut.

Front Fringe

Miscellaneous Beads

2.5 mm Gold Filled
3 mm Gold Filled
6 mm Rose Quartz

6 mm Two-Tone Rose Diamond

7x9 mm Two-Tone Rose Oval

6 mm Two-Tone Rose, Round

8 mm Clear Austrian Crystal

4 mm Clear Austrian Crystal

8x10 mm Dark Rose W/Flower

11x18 mm Antique Gold Flower Teardrop

7 mm Antique Gold Flower

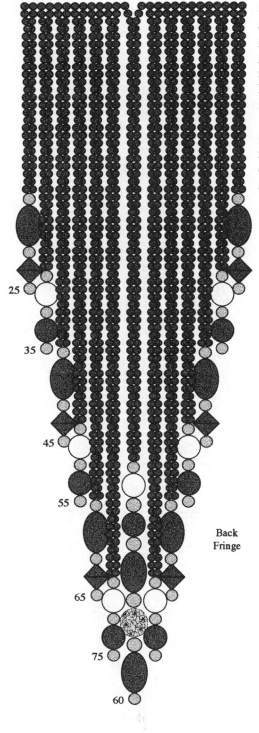

String A (misc. & 21 DB) on first needle and thread. With second needle and thread go through misc. beads, add one DB bead, go through next DB, add one, go through next. Repeat until a total of 11 DB beads have been added in-between. Peyote style strap explained on page 22.

String B (misc. & 323 DB). String A in reverse order (see page 24). Attach to other side corners of purse. Weave in same as first ends, cut.

Back Fringe

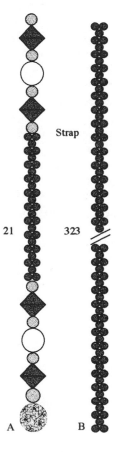

Strap

21

323

A

B

Pheasant Purse

Brick Stitch

Materials Needed ***

12 Colors of Delica
51 2.5 mm Gold Filled
64 3 mm Gold Filled
30 6 mm Gold Horn
 1 6x8 mm Rectangle Gold Horn
20 4x8 mm Red Horn
 2 4 mm Clear Red
16 6 mm Antique Gold Rosebud
10 6 mm Copper Rosebud
 9 7x9 mm Amethyst
 1 8x15 mm Antique Accent
     White Size D Nymo® Thread

Start 6th row down from the top. Base row is **58** beads (29 front beads, and 29 back done in DB 54 Lined Peach AB). See instructions for purse brick stitch, page 15. Work to top and add 3-bead lace edge (*Figure 16-a*). Weave end of thread in securely, cut.

Attach needle to other end of the thread. Continue with the rest of design, working in new sections of thread as needed. Stitch bottom of purse closed (*Figure 16-c*).

Front Fringe Attach 1 1/2 yard section of thread to front bottom corner of purse where shown on opposite page. Follow illustration on page 34.

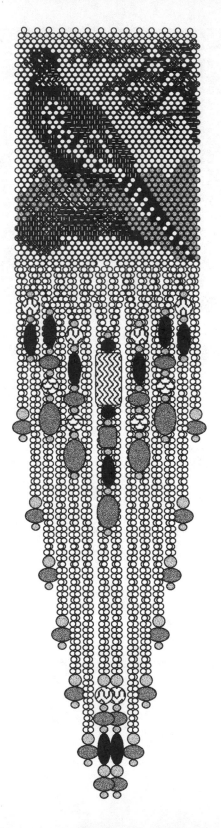

Mountain Village Purse
Mountain Bouquet Earrings
Bluebird Purse

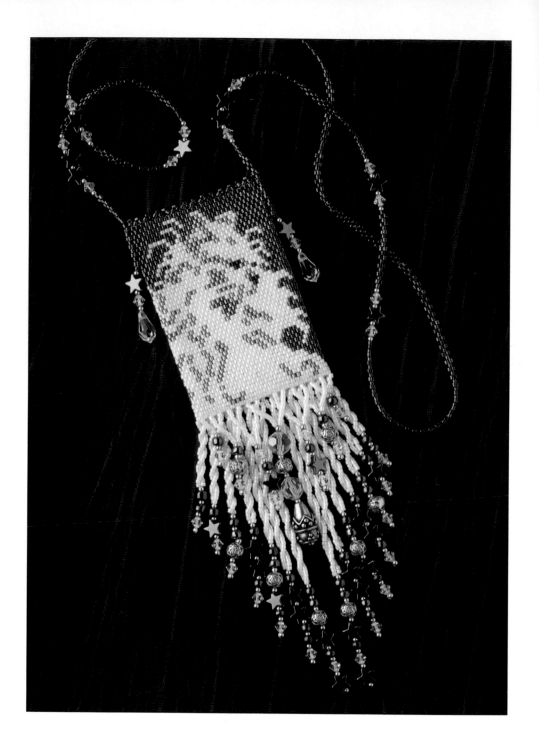

White Persian Cat Purse

Bouquet Purse
Bouquet Earrings

Sparrow Hawk Purse

Pheasant Purse

Star Purse & Mini Frosted Purse
Daisy Chain Necklace
Crocheted Cord Key Chain

Crocheted Cord Key Chain
Crocheted Necklace
Double Daisy Chain Bracelet

Hummingbird Purse
Hummingbird Earrings
Hummingbird Ornament

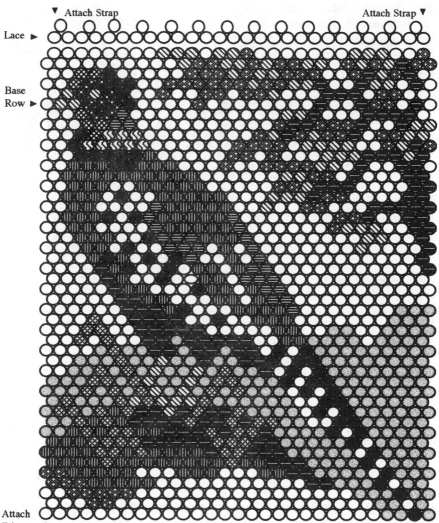

▼ Attach Strap   Attach Strap ▼

Lace ►

Base
Row ►

Attach
Fringe ▲

► 58 Base Row
46 Rows Long

○	DB 54 Lined Peach AB	⊜	DB 859 Matte Trans. Emerald AB
▥	DB 773 Matte Trans. Cherrywood	⊙	DB 791 Dyed Matte Opaque Red
◉	DB 857 Matte Tr. Lt. Amethyst AB	⊛	DB 29 Metallic Med. Bronze Iris
⊖	DB 23 Metallic Lt. Bronze Iris Cut	●	DB 25 Metallic Blue Iris
◈	DB 681 S/L Semi-Matte Squash	▩	DB 686 S/L Semi-Matte Jonquil
▦	AQ 562 Galvanized Tangerine	⊘	DB 201 White Pearl

33

1. Pick up 5 peach DB beads, add misc. beads, go back through misc. beads, add 5 more peach. Go up through 5th bead over along bottom of purse, out 3rd bead making sure thread is in front of last loop.

2. Pick up 8 peach, add misc. beads, go back through misc. beads, add 8 more peach. Go up through 9th bead over, out 7th again making sure thread is in front of last loop.

3. Add 10 peach, misc., 10 peach. Up 13th, out 11th, thread in front of last loop.

4. Add 12 peach, misc., 12 peach. Up 19th, out 17th. From this time on, the thread will be <u>behind</u> the previous loop.

5. 10 peach, misc., peach. Up 23, out 21.

6. 8 peach, misc., peach. Up 27 out 25.

7. 5 peach, misc., peach. Up 29. Weave in thread and cut.

Back Fringe Attach 4 yards of thread to the back, lower corner of purse. Follow illustration on opposite page.

Pick up 25 peach DB beads, add misc. beads, go back through misc. beads, add 25 peach beads. Twist (page 21), go up one bead over along bottom of purse. Continue rest of fringe in same way.

Pay attention to where two center fringe are connected to purse. Weave in end of thread, cut.

24" Strap Cut 2 sections of thread 1 yard each. Attach where shown, one thread in front corner, the other in back corner. Weave in ends at least one third way down purse, cut.

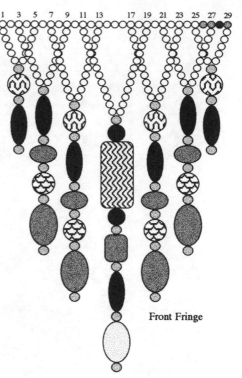

Front Fringe

Attach needles to other ends of thread. String A, B, C & D. String C, B & A in reverse (page 24). Twist strap (page 27), attach to other top corner of purse. Weave in one third way down purse, cut.

Miscellaneous Beads

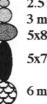

2.5 mm Gold Filled
3 mm Gold Filled
5x8 mm Red Horn

5x7 mm Gold Horn

6 mm Antique Gold Rosebud

6 mm Copper Rosebud

8x10 mm Amethyst

8x15 mm Antique Gold Accent

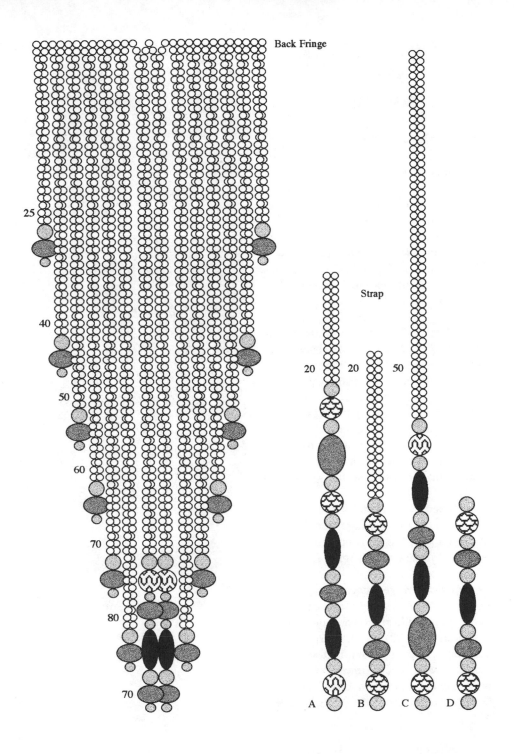

Back Fringe

Strap

A B C D

35

Sparrow Hawk Purse

Brick Stitch

Materials Needed ***

15 Colors of Delica
77 3 mm Gold Filled
13 2 mm Gold Filled
 9 5x7 mm Gold Horn
13 6 mm Clear Lt. Blue
11 4x7 mm Rectangle Amethyst
13 4x7 mm Tortoise Shell Color
17 6x11 mm Antique Gold Accent
     White Size D Nymo® Thread

Start 6th row down from top. Base row is 54 beads (27 front beads, and 27 back done in DB 203, Ceylon Lt. Yellow). See instructions for purse brick stitch, page 15. Work to top, add lace edge *(Figure 16-a)* along with stick fringe (a), (b), (a), instructions on page 22, illustration with bead count on page 38. Pine cone (c), over top of (b) where shown with small arrows. Weave end of thread in securely, cut.

Attach needle to other end of thread. Continue with the rest of design working in a new section of thread as needed. Stitch bottom of purse closed *(Figure 16-c)*.

Front Stick Fringe Attach a 2 yard section of thread to lower left front corner of purse. Follow illustration on page 38 (instructions page 22) for stick fringe and pine cones. Add fringe along bottom where indicated with small arrows on opposite page. Taper to point with A, B, C, D, E, F, G, H. Taper back up with G, F, E, D, C, B, A.

√ Use black permanent marker to darken threads showing on all Metallic Teal Iris stick fringe tips.

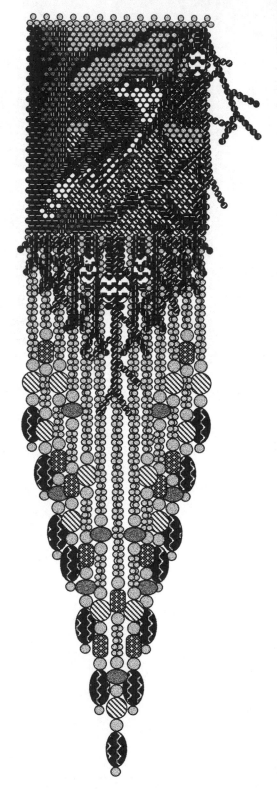

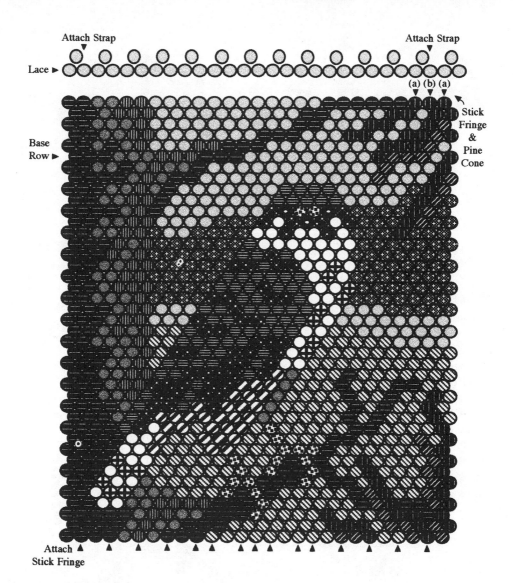

▶ 54 Base Row
41 Rows Long

● DB 10 Black		⊕ DB 686 Semi-Matte S/L Jonquil	
◉ DB 121 Dark Topaz Gold Luster		◐ DB 325 Matte Metallic Blue Iris	
⦀ DB 54 Lined Peach AB		⊜ DB 792 Dyed Matte Opaque Blue Grey	
○ DB 201 White Pearl		⊖ DB 23 Metallic Lt. Bronze Iris Cut	
◯ DB 203 Ceylon Light Yellow		⊗ DB 857 Matte Trans. Lt. Amethyst AB	
▯ DB 27 Metallic Teal Iris		⊘ DB 272 Lined Topaz/Yellow AB	
◑ DB 124 Trans. Chartreuse Luster		⊗ DB 692 Semi-Matte S/L Sky Blue	
		⊕ DB 25 Metallic Blue Iris	

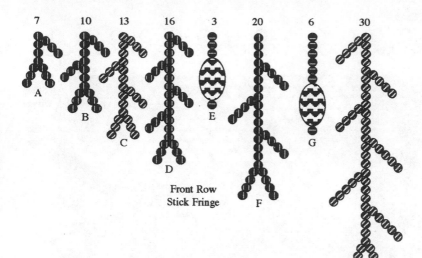

<table>
<tr><td>7</td><td>10</td><td>13</td><td>16</td><td>3</td><td>20</td><td>6</td><td>30</td></tr>
</table>

A B C D E F

Front Row
Stick Fringe

Back Fringe Weave into lower left corner a 3 yard section of thread. Pick up 20 DB 203, misc. beads, go back through misc. beads, add 20 DB 203, twist fringe (page 21), up purse 2nd bead over and down 3rd bead over. Pick up 15 DB 203, misc. beads, 5 DB 203, misc. beads. Go back through first misc. beads, add 5 DB 203, through next misc. beads, add 15 DB 203, twist fringe, up 4th bead over from corner, down 5th. Repeat following illustration on opposite page. Skip center bead of purse when attaching. Weave in end, cut.

Miscellaneous Beads

2 mm Gold Filled

3 mm Gold Filled

4x7 mm Amethyst

6 mm Clear Lt. Blue

5x7 mm Gold Horn

6x11 mm Antique Gold Accent

4x7 mm Tortoise Shell Color

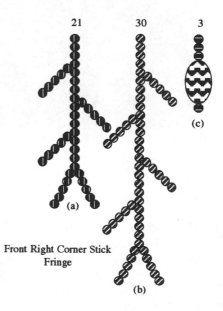

<table>
<tr><td>21</td><td>30</td><td>3</td></tr>
</table>

(a)

(b)

(c)

Front Right Corner Stick
Fringe

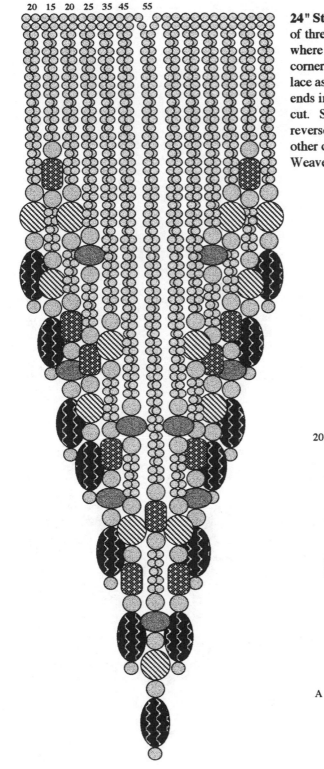

20 15 20 25 35 45 55

24" Strap Attach 2, 1 yard sections of thread to the upper purse corner where shown , 2nd bead over from corner front and back (go through lace as shown on page 37). Weave ends in one third way down purse, cut. String A, B & C . String in reverse B & A (page 24). Attach to other corner of purse in same way. Weave ends in, cut.

Strap

20   200

A   B   C

Canadian Geese Purse

Brick Stitch

Materials Needed **

    8 Colors of Delica
   23 3 mm Gold Filled
   65 2.5 mm Gold Filled
   15 2 mm Gold Filled
   27 4 mm Black Horn
   42 4 mm Matte Purple AB
    2 8 mm Round Bone
   19 5x9 mm Bone
   17 4x7 mm Tortoise Shell Color
       White Size D Nymo® Thread

Start 6th row down from top. Base row is 60 beads (30 front beads and 30 back done in DB 857, Matte Trans. Lt. Amethyst AB), see page 15.   Work to top, add lace edge (*Figure 16-a*). Weave end of thread in securely, cut.

Attach needle to the other end of thread. Continue with rest of design working in a new section of thread as needed. Stitch bottom of purse closed (*Figure 16-c*).

Front Stick Fringe Attach a 3 1/3 yard section of thread to lower *right* front section of purse where shown. Follow instructions on page 22 for stick fringe. Add fringe along bottom where indicated with small arrows shown on page 41. Refer to illustration on page 43 for bead count.

Add the last two stick fringe on body of purse where shown with white X's. Weave thread in and cut.

√ Use black permanent marker to darken threads showing at ends of all Metallic Blue Iris stick fringe.

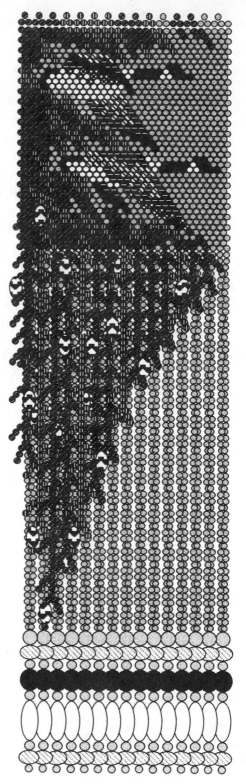

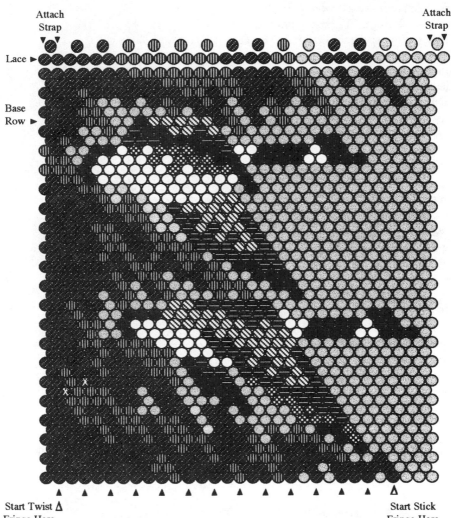

Attach Strap

Attach Strap

Lace ▶

Base Row ▶

Start Twist Δ
Fringe Here

Start Stick
Fringe Here

▶ 60 Base Row
43 Rows Long

◐	DB 857 Matte Tr. Lt. Amethyst AB	○	DB 203 Ceylon Lt. Yellow
●	DB 25 Metallic Blue Iris	◍	DB 697 Semi-Matte S/L Grey
⦀	DB 85 Lined Blue/Blue AB	⊖	DB 325 Matte Metallic Blue Iris
●	DB 10 Black	⊕	DB 121 Dark Topaz Luster

41

Back Fringe This fringe is all the same length, which makes it more difficult than the tapered fringe. The bead count may be a little over or under the 60 DB 857 beads depending on their consistency. Take the fringe out and redo it until you are happy. There is a lot of work to this purse, and making the fringe as even as possible is very important. See twist fringe instructions, page 21.

Weave into lower left corner, where indicated on page 41, a 4 yard section of thread. Pick up 60 DB 857, misc. beads, go back through misc. beads, add 60 DB 857, twist (see illustration to right). Go up purse 2nd bead over and down 3rd bead. Repeat for a total of 15 fringe. Weave in end, cut.

24" Strap Attach 2, 1 yard sections of thread to upper corners of purse where shown. The "V" at the end of the straps straddle a lace loop. Weave ends of thread into purse at least one third of the way down, cut. This is a peyote style strap, see page 22 for instructions. String A, B, C & D (245 actual beads). String in reverse C, B & A (page 24). Attach to other corner of purse in same way. Weave ends in, cut.

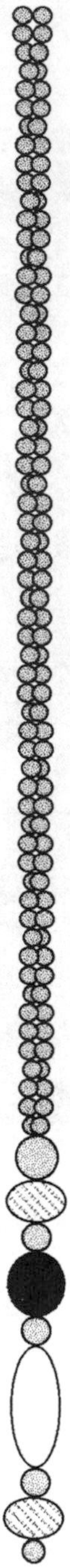

Back Twist
Fringe

Miscellaneous Beads

3 mm Gold Filled
2.5 mm Gold Filled
2 mm Gold Filled

4 mm Black Horn

4 mm Matte Purple AB

8 mm Bone

5x9 mm Bone

4x7 mm Tortoise Shell Color

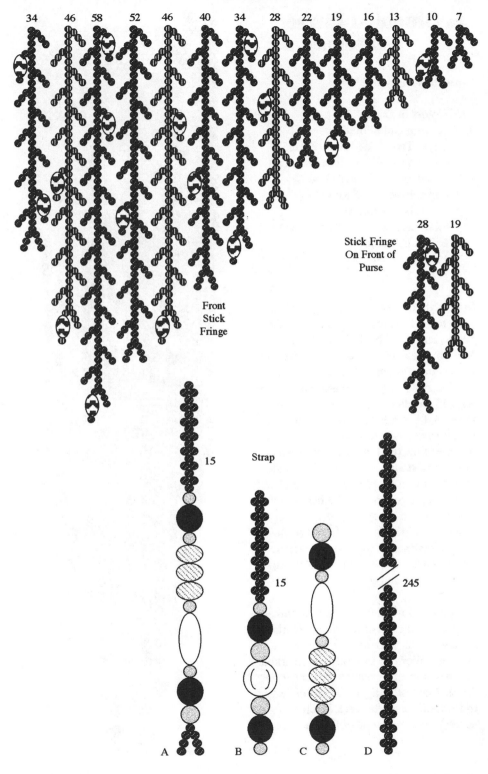

34 46 58 52 46 40 34 28 22 19 16 13 10 7

Front
Stick
Fringe

Stick Fringe
On Front of
Purse

28 19

15

Strap

15

245

A B C D

43

Bluebird Purse

Brick Stitch

Materials Needed ***

- 15 Colors of Delica
- 127 2.5 mm Gold Filled
- 1 6 mm Two-Toned Rose Round
- 21 6 mm Two-Toned Rose Diamond
- 17 6x8 mm Two-Toned Oval
- 33 4 mm Royal Blue Round
- 5 6 mm Blue Cloisonne
- 1 8x10 mm Rose W/Flower
- 19 6x7 mm Antique Gold
   Mushroom Spirals
   White Size D Nymo® Thread

Start 12th row down from top (6 full rows from top). Base row is 54 beads (29 front beads, and 25 in back done with DB 27, Metallic Teal Iris). See instructions on brick stitch for purses, page 15. Work to top full row. Start decreasing as shown with 17 beads for first row. Next rows have 14, 11, 8, 5 & 2. Leave 10 spaces and repeat rows. Add lace as shown, coming out one of the two top beads, go down end bead of next step, out bead of next step, repeat once more. Come out closest bead to last staggered row, add 3 beads, down next bead over, up next bead, add 3 beads, down, up, add 3, skip 1 bead and go down next. Finish across top and stair step up to top 2 beads. Repeat for back of purse. Weave in end and cut.

Attach needle to the other end of thread. Continue with rest of the design working in new 2 1/2 yard sections of thread as needed. Work to last full row marked. Stitch bottom of the purse together (*Figure 16-c*). Add last 3 staggered rows of design to front of purse (the back is left straight across). Weave in end of thread and cut.

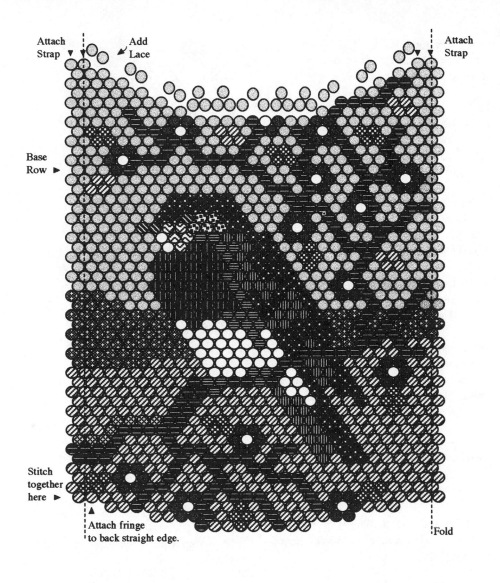

Attach Strap
Add Lace
Attach Strap
Base Row ▶
Stitch together here ▶
Attach fringe to back straight edge.
Fold

▶ 54 Base Row
43 Rows Long

DB 747	Matte Trans. Light Blue	DB 693	Semi-Matte S/L Med. Blue
DB 124	Trans. Chartreuse Luster	DB 774	Dyed Matte Trans. Red
DB 23	Met. Lt. Bronze Iris, Cut	DB 121	Dark Topaz Gold Luster
DB 685	Semi-Matte S/L Dark. Rose	DB 272	Lined Topaz/Yellow AB
DB 741	Matte Trans. Crystal	DB 864	Matte Trans. Cobalt AB
DB 27	Metallic Teal Iris	DB 252	Ceylon Grey
DB 857	Matte Tr. Lt. Amethyst AB	DB 10	Black
		DB 697	Semi-Matte S/L Grey

45

Front Fringe Attach a 1 1/2 yard section of thread to the front bottom staggered edge.

1. Pick up 2 DB 124 (Trans. Chartreuse Luster), add misc. beads, go back through misc. beads, add 2 more DB 124. Go up through third bead over on row, down through bead end of next row below.

2. Pick up 3 DB 124, misc. beads, go back through misc. beads, add 3 DB, up through third bead over on row and down through the end bead of the bottom row.

3. Pick up 9 DB, up through third bead over, down through next. Create 2 more loops. Last 2 loops will be added later.

4. Go back down 4 of the beads in the last loop just added. Pick up 3 DB, misc., up through misc. and the 3 DB. Finish off center of front fringe following instructions on page 54 for lattice style fringe.

5. After adding the longest center fringe, go back up through the lattice and come out to finish the last 2 loops along the right bottom edge. Weave in end and cut.

Back Fringe Attach 3 yards of thread to the lower back corner of the purse (shown on page 45).

Pick up 25 DB 124 beads (Trans. Chartreuse Luster), add misc. beads, go back through misc. beads, add 25 DB. Twist (see page 21), hold thread next to beads to keep from losing twists, go up one bead over along bottom of purse. Continue rest of fringe in same fashion.

Pay attention to how the center fringe is attached. Weave in end of thread, cut.

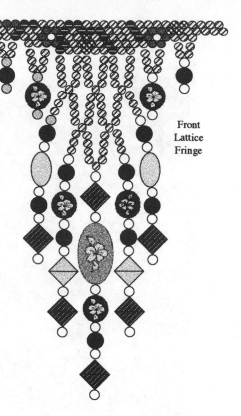

Front Lattice Fringe

Miscellaneous Beads

2.5 mm Gold Filled

6 mm Two-Tone Rose Round

6 mm Multi-Tone Rose Diamond

6x8 mm Two-Ton Oval

4 mm Matte Royal Blue

6 mm Blue Cloisonne

8x10 mm Rose W/Flower

6x7 mm Antique Gold Mushroom Spiral

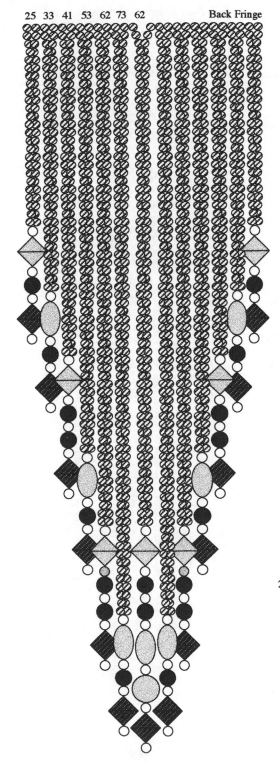

25 33 41 53 62 73 62   Back Fringe

attached. Weave in end of thread, cut.

24" Strap Cut 2 sections of thread 1 yard each. Attach where shown on page 45. Weave in ends at least one third way down purse to secure, cut.

String A, B, C & D, then C, B & A in reverse (see page 24). Follow instructions on page 22 for peyote style strap. Attach to other corner of purse where shown. Weave in ends of the thread at least one third down to secure, cut.

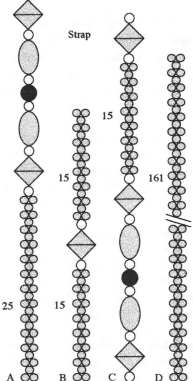

Strap

15

15

161

25

15

15

A   B   C   D

White Persian Cat Purse

Brick Stitch

Materials **

- 5 Colors of Delica
- 143 2 mm Sterling Silver
- 28 6 mm Hemalyke Stars
- 36 4 mm Clear Austrian Crystal
- 38 4 mm Round Hemalyke
- 2 5x11 mm Clear Teardrop Crystals
- 9 6 mm Silver Rosebud
- 1 7x10 mm Silver Accent
   White Size D Nymo® Thread

Start 6th row down from top. Base row is 58 beads (31 front, 27 in back done with DB 201, White Pearl). See instructions on brick stitch for purses, page 15. Work to top, add lace edge (*Figure 16-a*). Weave end of thread in securely, cut.

Attach needle to the other end of the thread. Continue with the rest of design, working in 2 1/2 yard sections of thread as needed. Stitch bottom of purse closed (*Figure 16-c*).

Front Fringe Attach 1 1/2 yard section of thread to the front bottom corner of the purse where shown on page 49. Work short end of thread into purse to secure. Create loops across the bottom edge of purse starting at number 1. Follow instructions on page 34 for Pheasant Purse front fringe using the color and count of beads shown on page 50. Weave end of thread into purse to secure, cut.

Back Fringe Attach 3 yards of thread to the back, lower corner of purse. Follow illustration on page 51, using instructions on page 21 for back twist fringe.

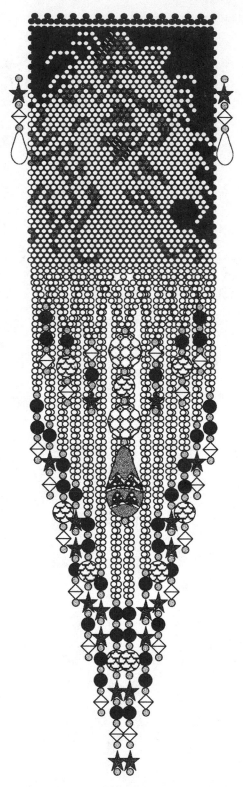

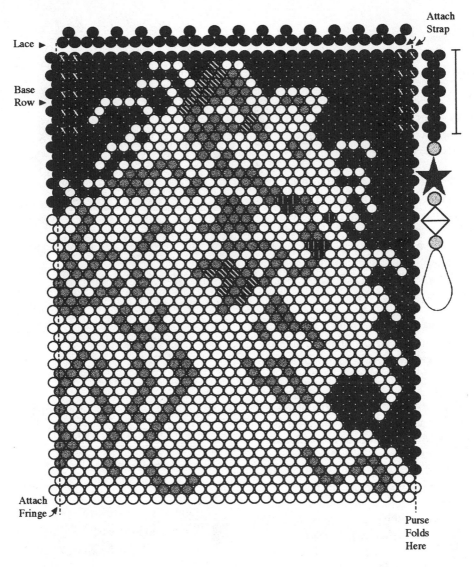

Lace ►

**Base
Row ►**

**Attach
Strap**

**Attach
Fringe**

**Purse
Folds
Here**

► 58 Base Row
  50 Row Long

○ DB 201 White Pearl
● DB 25 Metallic Blue Iris
◉ DB 697 Semi-Matte S/L Grey
◓ DB   1 Gunmetal
◐ DB 10 Black

49

24" Strap *This strap is done a bit differently. It is constructed first before it is attached.

Cut 2 sections of thread 1 1/2 yard each. Start the beads 9" from end leaving the long tail for sewing the strap to the purse later.

√ To save threading time, use 4 needles, 1 on each end of two sections of thread.

Follow instructions on page 22 for peyote style strap, using the illustration on page 51. String A, B, C & D. String C, B & A in reverse (see page 24).

Attach teardrop crystal with both threads, shown below. Go back up through misc. beads at end of strap to first 2 DB beads marked with arrow.

√ These crystals have a horizontal hole which can cut thread. Use clear nail polish to hold thread in place, let dry. Another choice is to use crystal with a vertical hole along with a small bead at bottom to hold crystal in place. Go through that bead with both threads, back up through misc. beads and continue with instructions below.

Attach to the two lowest DB beads shown with white X's on page 49. Work from bottom, up. Run both threads up through single DB bead on strap then attach to next two X's. Repeat for a total of 5 times. Work the ends of thread into the body of purse, cut. Repeat on other end of strap.

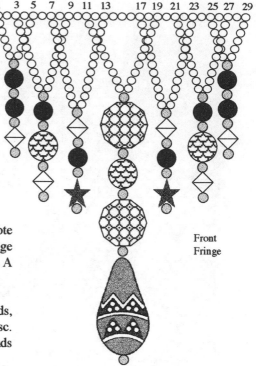

Front Fringe

Miscellaneous Beads

2 mm Sterling Silver

6 mm Hemalyke Star

4 mm Clear Austrian Crystal

4 mm Round Hemalyke

5x11 mm Clear Teardrop Crystal

6 mm Silver Rosebud

8 mm Clear Crystal, AB

7x10 mm Silver Accent

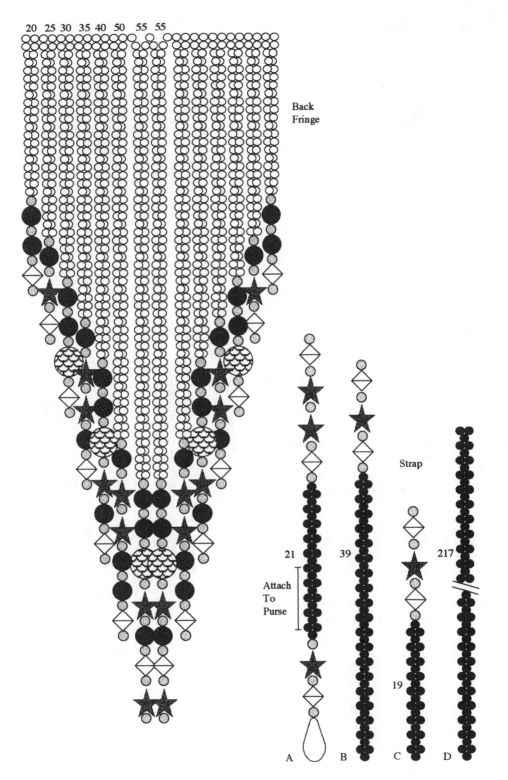

20 25 30 35 40 50 55 55

Back
Fringe

Strap

21

Attach
To
Purse

39

217

19

A   B   C   D

51

Hummingbird Purse
Vertical Brick Stitch

Materials Needed *

10 Colors of Delica
42 2 mm Gold Filled
 4 3 mm Gold Filled
23 5 x 9 mm Chartreuse
    White Size D Nymo® Thread

This purse was created using brick stitch running vertically. In appearance, it looks just like peyote, but it is done completely different. Follow instructions on page 16.

Left Half Start where marked with arrow for base row. The base row goes from the top of the front to top of the back (28 front, 28 back done in DB 203, Ceylon Light Yellow). Continue to left edge of purse attaching thread as needed. Weave end in securely. If there is still remaining thread, leave for stitching up the side later.

Right Half Attach needle to remainder of first section of thread and finish right half. Use any remaining thread to stitch up the side, or attach a new section for this purpose.

There are thread loops along the side edge of both last rows. Fold the front and back halves together and stitch through these loops as shown below. A double loop of thread at each end will help to re-inforce. Weave in tail of thread securely, cut.

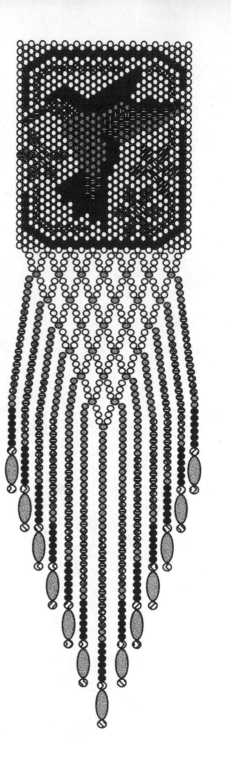

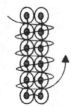

▼ Attach Strap   Base Row   Attach Strap ▼

Attach Fringe ▲

▼ 56 Base Row
31 Rows Wide

○	DB 203 Ceylon Lt. Yellow		◐	DB 681 S/L Semi-Matte Squash
◉	DB 124 Trans. Chartreuse Luster		◑	DB 685 S/L Semi-Matte Dark Rose
●	DB 27 Metallic Teal Iris		◉	DB 684 S/L Semi-Matte Med. Rose
⊗	AQ 564 Metallic Russet		⊖	DB 25 Metallic Blue Iris
⊜	DB 54 Lined Peach AB		⊜	DB 121 Dark Topaz Gold Luster

Lattice Fringe Attach a 3 yard section of thread to the bottom corner of the purse where shown on page 53. Weave short end into purse securely and cut. Follow illustration for lattice fringe below.

1. Add three DB 203, one DB 124, and three DB 203. Connect to bottom edge of purse where shown below with arrows on page 53..
2. Repeat for a total of 7 small loops.
3. Go back through the last three DB 203, add dangle fringe as shown. Go back through dangle and single DB 124 in the loop.
4. Add 6 loops and dangle. Go down through three beads of last loop, add dange fringe, go back through dangle and single DB 124 in the loop.
5. Repeat until tapered to one loop with dangle fringe in center.
6. Work way back through fringe and into bag. Weave thread in securely, cut.

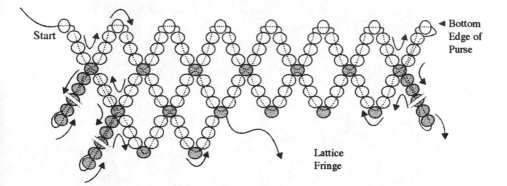

Start

Bottom
Edge of
Purse

Lattice
Fringe

24" Strap Cut 2 sections of thread, 1 yard each. Attach where shown on page 53, one thread in front corner of purse and one in back corner. Weave in both threads at least one third way down. Connect needles to other ends of thread and follow illustration at right. String A, B, C, D & E. String D, C, B & A in reverse (see page 24). See instructions on page 22 for peyote style strap. Twist strap (page 27), attach to other side corners of purse. Weave in same as other side, cut.

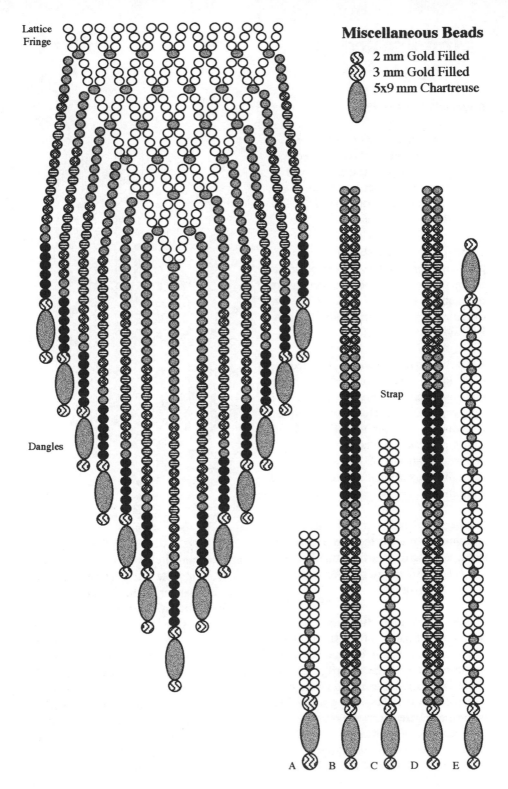

Lattice
Fringe

Miscellaneous Beads

2 mm Gold Filled
3 mm Gold Filled
5x9 mm Chartreuse

Strap

Dangles

A   B   C   D   E

Mini Frosted Purse
Right Angle Weave

Materials Needed **

11/o Matte Transparent Crystal Seed
11/o Lt. Rose Opalescent Gilt-Lined Seed
11/o Lavender Opalescent Gilt-Lined
  3   4 mm Clear Austrian Crystal
  1   5x11 mm Teardrop Crystal
      White Size D Nymo® Thread

Front Start where shown on opposite page with approximately 3 yards of thread. Use guide provided. See instructions for right angle weave on pages 17 & 18. Complete 13 circles of beads, 13 rows. Put aside, do not tie off.

Back Start at bottom where indicated and work up 13 rows. Reposition for flap (*always in curves, never straight). Add 3 squares, turn. Repeat for a total of 6 times. Decrease down to one square. Add bead, teardrop crystal, another bead and back into single square of beads. Go back through flap working in end, tie off and work in tail.

Connecting Hold front and back together and connect by using the same right angle stitch and inserting the beads marked with x's (*Figure 57-a*). Start at top and work around to top of other side.

Fringe Attach approximately 2 yards of thread to left corner of the front section where shown. Complete one more full length row, then decrease (page 18) one circle of beads on each side, one row. Complete the first dangle by going across with three circles, turn and repeat. Next row, decrease to one circle. Add bead, crystal, three beads, back through the crystal, add another bead and back into

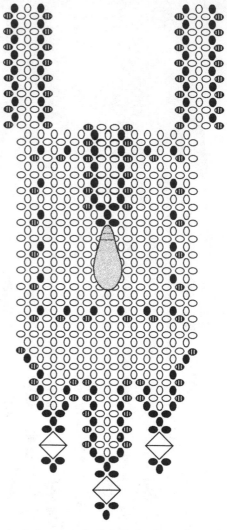

single bottom circle. Go back up through dangle. Complete second and third dangle in same manner making center dangle longer, as shown. Work in about 4 inches of thread to secure, cut.

24" Strap Attach where shown. About 5 yards of thread will be needed for each strap. Complete 94 rows of 3 circles each or 12 inches. Attach a double cup bead tip and bead (*Figure 76-e*) to the end bead of center circle, jump ring and clasp. Repeat for other side. Work in ends, tie off and cut.

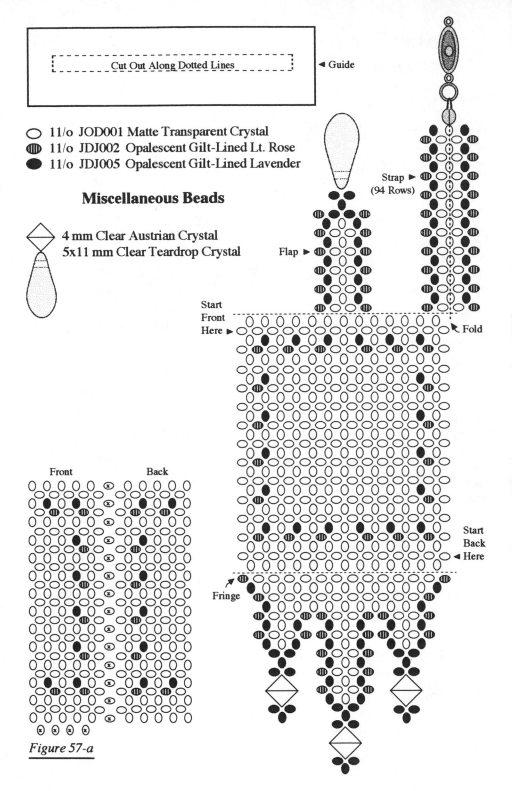

Cut Out Along Dotted Lines ◄ Guide

○ 11/o JOD001 Matte Transparent Crystal
◍ 11/o JDJ002 Opalescent Gilt-Lined Lt. Rose
● 11/o JDJ005 Opalescent Gilt-Lined Lavender

Miscellaneous Beads

4 mm Clear Austrian Crystal
5x11 mm Clear Teardrop Crystal

Strap ►
(94 Rows)

Flap ►

Start
Front
Here ►

◄ Fold

Front   Back

Figure 57-a

Start
Back
◄ Here

Fringe

Star Purse

Herringbone Weave

Materials *****

11/o White Opalescent Gilt-Lined Seed
62   2 mm Gold Filled
 6   3 mm Gold Filled
25   6 mm Antique Gold Rosebud
18   Small Gold Star Charms
     White Size D Nymo® Thread

Front Start with approximately 3 yards of thread at the top edge of the pattern shown on the opposite page. String 36 beads for 18 bead wide purse. Follow instructions on pages 19 & 20 for Herringbone Weave. Decrease along bottom as shown. Work in about 3 inches of tail, cut.

Back Work the same as the front other than at the beginning, start beads approximately 1 yard in on the thread. This thread will be used later for adding the flap.

Flap Make a 6 bead wide flap, 14 rows long. For Flap fringe, pick up 5 seed beads, 3 mm gold filled bead, rosebud bead, 3 mm gold filled bead and 15 seed. Go around 15th seed, back through rest of seed, misc. beads, back into end bead of flap and out next bead over. Follow illustration for the rest of flap fringe. Work in about 3 inches tail of thread to secure, cut.

Weave in a new section of thread and sew front, bottom and back together. Work in end and cut.

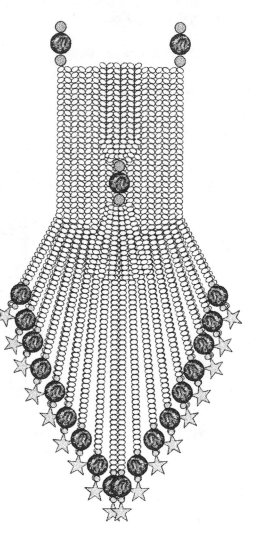

○   11/o JDJ001 Gild-Lined White Opalescent

Miscellaneous Beads

2 mm Gold Filled
3 mm Gold Filled
6 mm Antique Gold Rosebud

Small Gold Star Charm

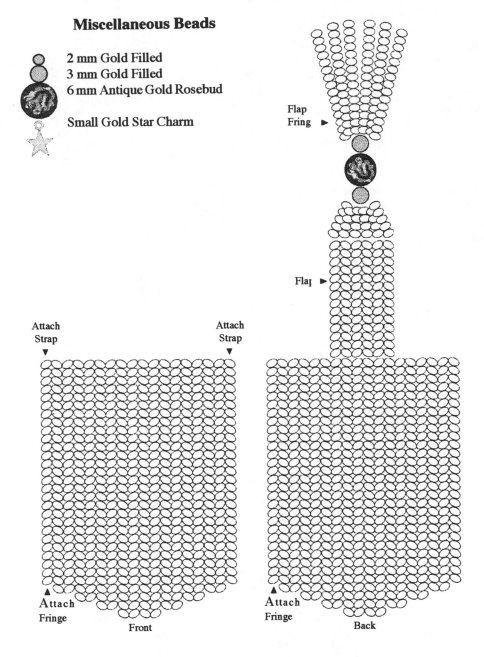

Flap
Fring ▶

Flap ▶

Attach
Strap
▼

Attach
Strap
▼

▲
Attach
Fringe

Front

Attach
Fringe

Back

Fringe There is a front row of fringe with rosebud beads along the bottom and a back row with stars. The back row fringe is approximately 5 seed beads longer than the front row fringe (follow illustration at right and below). Attach approximately 2 1/2 yards for front and same for back to lower left corner (front and back) where shown on page 59. Weave about 2-3 inches of thread into body of purse to secure. Do the same on other corner.

24" Strap Cut 2 sections of thread 1 yard each. Attach where shown in illustration on page 59, one thread in front corner, one in back corner. Work in tail of thread to secure, cut. Add A, B & C, then B & A in reverse (see page 24). Twist (page 27). Attach the 2 threads to the other corner of the purse, front and back. Work in tail of thread, cut.

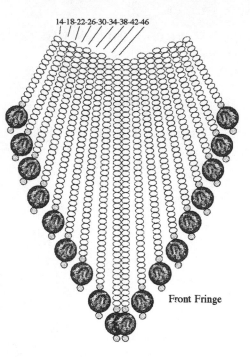

14-18-22-26-30-34-38-42-46

Front Fringe

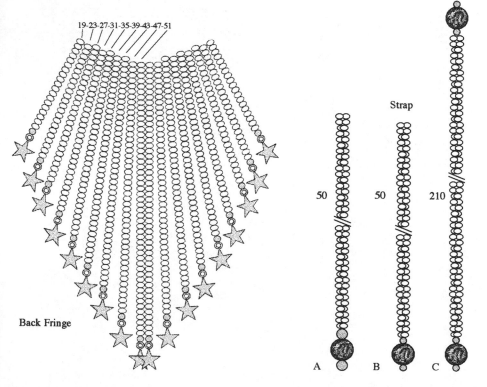

19-23-27-31-35-39-43-47-51

Back Fringe

Strap

50   50   210

A   B   C

Earrings & Ornament
Introduction

This chapter includes earrings to match three of the Amulet Purses found in the previous chapter. Two are horizontal brick stitch bouquets and the third is a vertical humming-bird.

The hummingbird has turned out to be quite versatile. Besides making a purse and earring design, it works great as an ornament. It can be hung by a window (not too much sun, though, beads can fade) letting the light pass through the clear chartreuse beads making it look like miniature stained glass.

The acrylic ornament, ribbon and braid used for this project can be purchased at craft or fabric stores. The ornament itself is not only good for hummingbirds. At Christmastime the Santa Claus pin, minus the leather and pin, make a great tree ornament. Also try candy canes, wreaths, the mallard duck taking off and the rearing horse. They have all worked well. All these designs can be found in my books **Beaded Images** & **Beaded Images II**, or try coming up with your own ideas.

Bouquet Earrings
Brick Stitch

Materials Needed **

- 7 Colors of Delica
- 22 2 mm Gold Filled
- 8 4 mm Clear Austrian Crystal
- 6 6 mm Two-Toned Diamond Shape
- 1 1/2 yards White Size O Nymo® Thread

Top Half Start with first two beads placed at 36 inches in on the thread (*Figure 11-a*). Begin at row (1) with base row of 9. Increase and decrease rows referring to pages 13 and 14 (*Figures a* through *d*).

Add the ear wire extension by going up through misc. beads, add <u>four</u> DB 25 and ear wire, down through misc. beads and into earring. Repeat for strength. Make sure to face second earring in opposite direction.

Bottom Half Attach needle to second half of thread. Start at (17), increasing by one bead. Continue through design.

Fringe Add to bottom of design where shown. Follow instructions on page 21 for twist fringe.

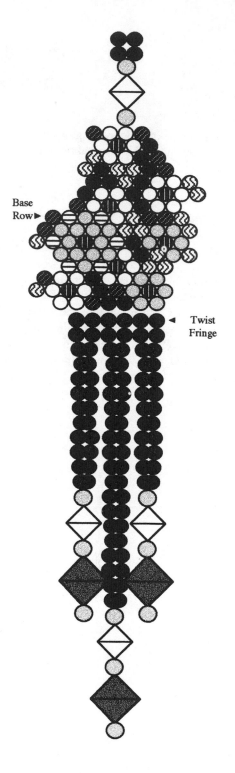

Base
Row▶

◄ Twist
Fringe

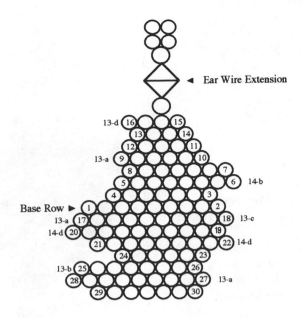

◄ Ear Wire Extension

13-d
13-a
14-b
Base Row ►
13-a
14-d
13-c
14-d
13-b
13-a

Miscellaneous Beads

● DB 25 Metallic Blue Iris
○ DB 201 White Pearl
◐ DB 27 Metallic Teal Iris
✖ DB 124 Tr. Chartreuse Luster
◑ DB 856 Matte Tr. Red Orange AB
⊜ DB 70 Lined Rose Pink
◍ DB 681 Semi-Matte S/L Squash

2 mm Gold Filled
4 mm Clear Austrian Crystal

6 mm Two-Toned Rose Diamond

63

Mountain Bouquet Earrings

Brick Stitch

Materials Needed **

5 Colors of Delica & Antique
12 3 mm Gold Filled
10 2 mm Gold Filled
 2 4 mm Red Jasper
 4 6 mm Antique Gold Rosebuds
 2 5x11 mm Teardrop Amethyst
1 1/2 yards White Size O Nymo® Thread

Top Half Start with first two beads placed at 22 inches in on the thread. Begin at (1) with base row of 9. Increase and decrease rows referring to pages 13 and 14 (*Figures a* through *d*).

Add the ear wire extension by going up through misc. beads, add <u>six</u> DB 27 and ear wire, down through misc. beads and into earring. Repeat for strength. Make sure to face second earring in opposite direction.

Bottom Half Attach the needle to second half of thread. Start at (15), increasing by one bead. Continue through design.

Fringe Add to bottom of design where shown. Tie off below large flower on right, cut.

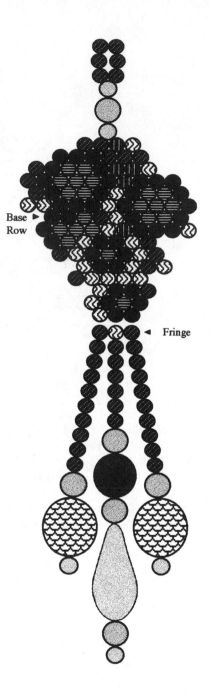

Base ▶
Row

◀ Fringe

64

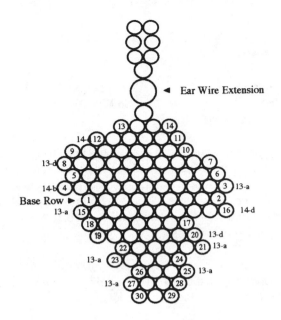

◄ Ear Wire Extension

13 14
14 12 11
9 10
13-d 8 7
5 6
14-b 4 3 13-a
Base Row ► 1 2
13-a 15 16 14-d
18 17
19 20 13-d
22 21 13-a
13-a 23 24
26 25 13-a
13-a 27 28
30 29

Miscellaneous Beads

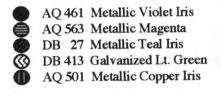

AQ 461 Metallic Violet Iris
AQ 563 Metallic Magenta
DB 27 Metallic Teal Iris
DB 413 Galvanized Lt. Green
AQ 501 Metallic Copper Iris

2 mm Gold Filled
3 mm Gold Filled

4 mm Red Jasper

6 mm Antique Gold Rosebud

5x11 mm Teardrop Amethyst

Hummingbird Earrings

Vertical Brick Stitch

Materials Needed ***

8 Colors Delica & Antique
14/o Clear Seed Beads
1 3/4 yards White Size O Nymo® Thread

4 mm Clear Austrian Crystal
11/o Metallic Green Seed Beads

Left Half Start with first two beads placed at 36 inches in on thread. Begin at (1) with base row of 9. At beginning of second row, add one AQ 1, Crystal (clear) bead (*Figure 13-a*). Continue, following numbers showing the beginning and end of each row. Increase and decrease referring to pages 13 and 14 (*Figures a* through *d*). *Note, left side of hummingbird's tail is completed before head is started. Curved arrows show what beads to go through when repositioning.

Beak Add first bead of beak (*Figure 67-a*). Start with thread marked with "x". Add second beak bead (*Figure 67-b*), then third (*Figure 67-c*). Exit where indicated with straight arrow on chest. Tie off on loop shown, cut.

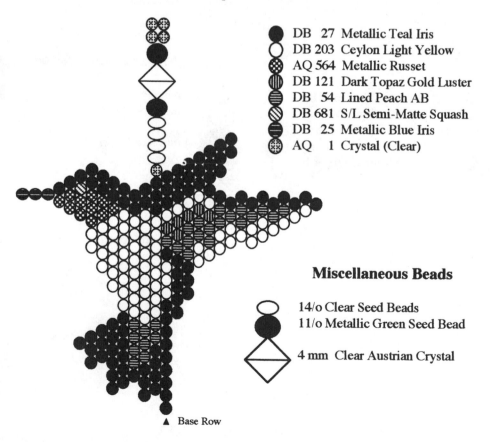

● DB 27 Metallic Teal Iris
○ DB 203 Ceylon Light Yellow
⊗ AQ 564 Metallic Russet
▥ DB 121 Dark Topaz Gold Luster
⊜ DB 54 Lined Peach AB
⊘ DB 681 S/L Semi-Matte Squash
⊖ DB 25 Metallic Blue Iris
⊛ AQ   1 Crystal (Clear)

▲ Base Row

Miscellaneous Beads

14/o Clear Seed Beads
11/o Metallic Green Seed Bead

4 mm Clear Austrian Crystal

Right Half Attach needle to other section of thread. Go up through beads and exit for beginning of row (35) position. *Note, top wing is completed before continuing with lower wing.

After wings are completed, follow dotted line to reposition coming out crystal (clear) AQ 1. Add ear wire extension going up through misc. beads, four DB beads, back through misc. beads, through AQ 1 bead in opposite direction and into bird body. Repeat for strength. Exit bird where indicated with straight arrow under lower wing. Tie off on loop shown, cut.

√ Add actual ear wires after the earrings are completed. It is difficult to tell which way the birds will face until completion. Make sure they face opposite directions. Use needle nose pliers, turn ear wire loop sideways, slip beaded extension loop over ear wire loop. With pliers, move ear wire loop back to original position. Be very careful of beads.

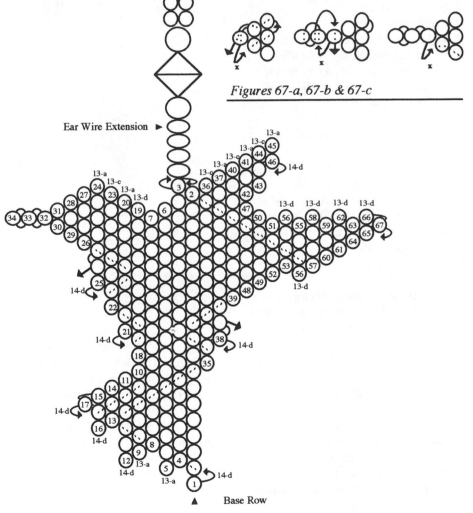

Figures 67-a, 67-b & 67-c

Ear Wire Extension ▶

Base Row

67

Hummingbird Ornament
Vertical Brick Stitch

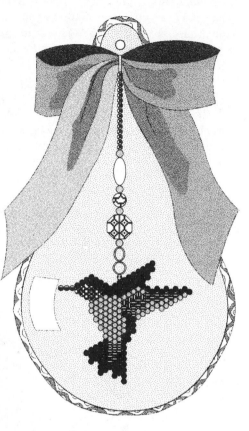

Materials Needed *

8 Colors of Delica
5 2 mm Gold Filled
1 8 mm Austrian Crystal AB
1 6 mm Antique Gold Rosebud
1 6x9 mm Chartreuse Oval
1 3" Gold Head Pin
1 6 mm Split Ring
1 9 mm Jump Ring
1 130 mm Acrylic Teardrop Ornament
   14" of 7/8" Burgundy/Gold Ribbon
   13" of 3/8" Burgundy/Gold Braid
   6" Gold Elastic Cord (for hanging)
   34 Gauge Gold Wire
   Glue Gun
1 3/4 yards White Size O Nymo® Thread

Follow instructions for the Hummingbird Earring on pages 66 & 67. Use DB 124, Lt. Chartreuse Luster, for the birds chest and wing trim instead of DB 203, Ceylon Lt. Yellow. Do not add extension for ear wire, just add crystal clear DB bead where shown and 6 mm split ring.

√ A split ring is used instead of a jump ring to prevent the thread from slipping through the cut a jump ring has.

√ Clear nail polish is painted on both sides of hummer to make it ridged and flat. It can otherwise bend when jarred against inside of ornament

The teardrop ornament comes in 2 halves. On one of the halves, approximately 3/4" down from the top, drill a 1/16" hole for the head pin. Take the 3" head pin, with needle nose pliers bend at 90 degree just below the head and insert pin into hole with the head on the outside of the ornament. Add beads as shown on page 70. Trim length of head pin wire if hummer looks like it will hang too low. Create a loop with round nose pliers at end of head pin to hang the hummingbird. Turn wire and hummer to where it faces even with the front, glue in place at inside top with glue gun.

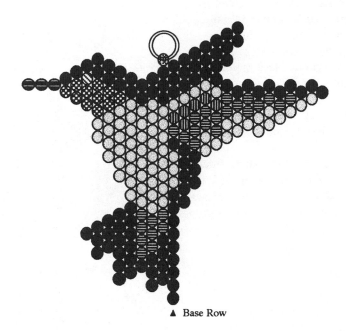

▲ Base Row

▲ 19 Base Row

● DB 27 Metallic Teal Iris	⊜ DB 54 Lined Peach AB
◑ DB 124 Trans. Chartreuse Luster	⊘ DB 681 S/L Semi-Matte Squash
⊛ AQ 564 Metallic Russet	⊜ DB 25 Metallic Blue Iris
⊜ DB 121 Dark Topaz Gold Luster	⊛ AQ 1 Crystal Clear

Cut a section of ribbon approximately 14" in length angling ends as show on next page. Create a bow by crossing ends as shown, crease and hold center with fingers. Slip 9 mm open jump ring over creased center area and squeeze shut.

√ Cut a 5" piece of 34 gauge gold wire and wrap around center just completed, twist close to ribbon. This will be wrapped around the top of the ornament after gluing bow on to insure bow does not come off.

Glue bow over top of head pin. Wrap 34 gauge wire around ornament and twist tight with needle nose pliers. Bring ends of wire back towards front. This will be covered with braid. Cut any excess.

Cut a section of braid to fit around the outside of the ornament approx. 12 1/2" long.

√ Braid ends tends to unravel easily. Wrap a small section of 34 gauge gold wire around the braid and twist tight with needle nose pliers just before length to be cut. Place another section of wire, done in same way, about 1/2" further. Cut in middle of 1/2" section and trim off excess wire. This will keep both ends from unraveling.

With both halves of ornament fitted together, start at center bottom and, using glue gun, attach braid over side seam. Attach 6" gold elastic cord for hanging.

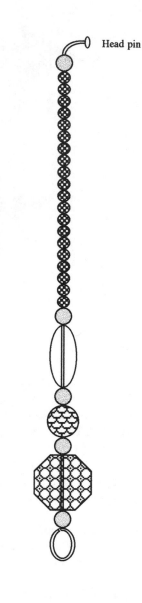

Head pin

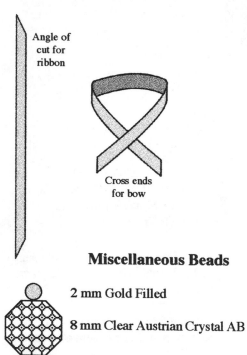

Angle of cut for ribbon

Cross ends for bow

Miscellaneous Beads

2 mm Gold Filled

8 mm Clear Austrian Crystal AB

6 mm Antique Gold Rosebud

5x9 mm Chartreuse Oval

Bracelets & Necklaces
Introduction

The first section of this chapter deals with crocheted cord bracelets, necklaces and key chains. These are a lot of fun to make once you get past the first few rows. Knowledge of crocheting is important. The hook used is small, making it difficult even for someone with crocheting experience. A booklet on the basics of crocheting can be found at a craft or fabric store. Chain and slip stitch are the only stitches used in these designs. This project is well worth the effort.

Upon first glance, the work could be mistaken for peyote stitch, as they look very much alike. Crocheting makes a more flexible piece, because each bead is independent of the next. It is so flexible the finished cord can be tied into a knot. The whole design is crocheted in a spiral, round and round until the desired length is reached. With practice, it goes much faster and is enjoyable to do, a nice change from other types of beading.

The rest of the chapter is on single daisy chain bracelets, necklaces and double daisy chain bracelets. They are fun and simple to make. The color combinations are endless. The single daisy chain can be made into wrist or ankle bracelets or necklaces, depending on the length. Seed beads work best. Double daisy chain bracelets are done in a peyote stitch, completely explained. They can look very different depending on what type of bead is used and are best done in bracelet form, as they do not contour correctly for ankle bracelets or necklaces.

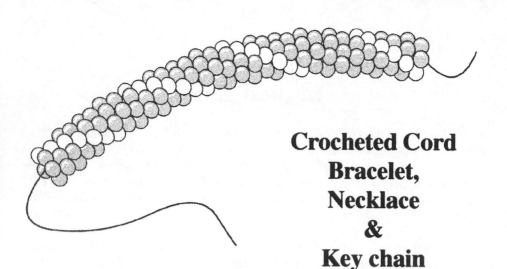

Crocheted Cord
Bracelet,
Necklace
&
Key chain

Materials Needed ****

 90 Seed beads per inch of cord crocheted (Two contrasting colors)
100 DB beads per inch of cord crocheted
  2 1 inch Eye Pin
  2 Bell Caps
  2 Jump Rings
  1 Clasp
Size 13 or 14 crochet hook
Size 12 English needle
Size D Nymo® Thread (Approx. 1 yard per inch crocheted)

Bracelet

Row One Measure and cut the length of thread needed. This can be a long piece and difficult to handle. I have worked with the thread still connected to the spool to make sure there is plenty. This can sometimes be cumbersome to haul around, but knots can be difficult to work into the beadwork if you run out. Waxing it is a matter of choice. It does not need to be done all at once. Waxed thread does make the crocheting easier. The wax creates drag on the thread allowing for better tension when run through the fingers.

String all the beads that are needed for the project at one time. This is especially important if the thread is not cut from the spool. The spiral design shown is easy to do. Just string four beads of one color and one of a contrasting color. Repeat, 4 - 1, until all beads needed are strung. The design spirals naturally as long as you crochet the same color bead over same color. A stop bead can be added on the end of the thread not being crocheted if it has been cut from the spool. This prevents the beads from slipping off the end not being used but is not always necessary.

With all the beads strung, start crocheting about 10 inches from the end. This leaves enough thread for the clasp to be added later.

With your crochet hook, chain five stitches (*Figure 73-a*), each time positioning the bead over the hook before pulling the thread through (*Figure 73-b*). Join to the first stitch with a slip stitch making a circle of five beads (*Figure 73-c*).

Second Row Push the hook through the loop of the first bead crocheted. Move this bead over to the right of the hook (*Figure 73-d*), this is important. Next make sure you bring the thread around and over the top of this bead (*Figure 73-e*), this is also very important. These two steps position the bead correctly. Slide a new bead into position and slip stitch. Make sure the contrasting bead is crocheted above the same. Continue in this fashion until desired length, making sure there are only five beads per row.

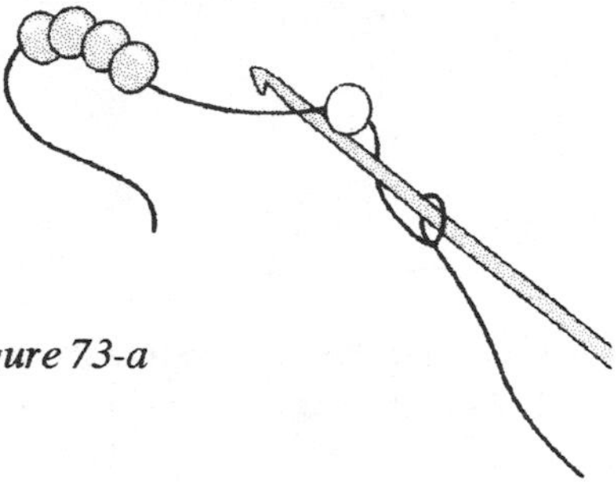

Figure 73-a

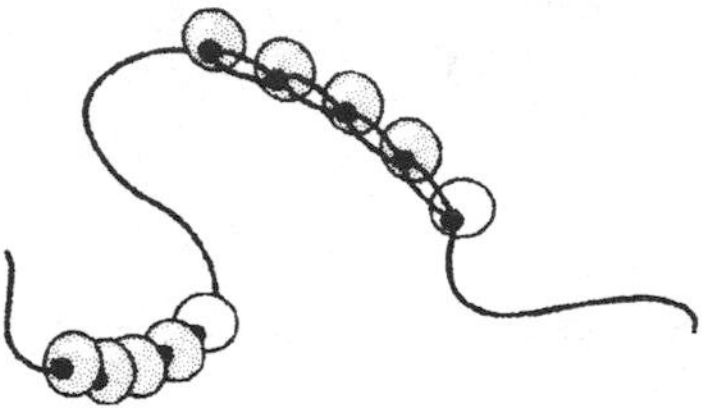

Figure 73-b

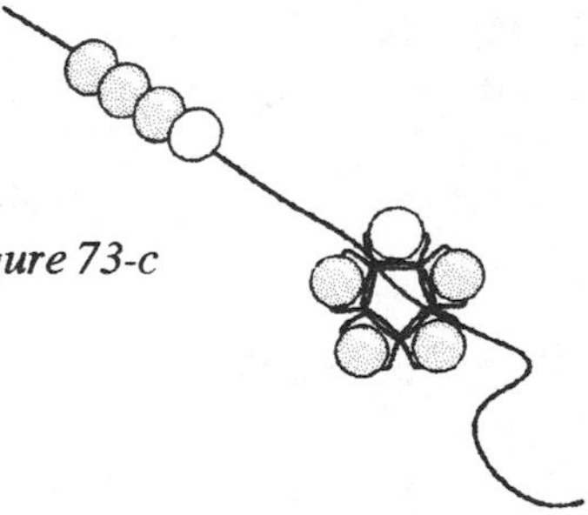

Figure 73-c

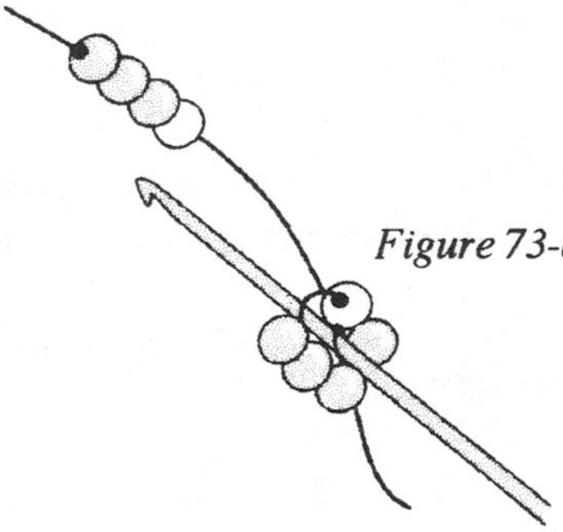

Figure 73-d

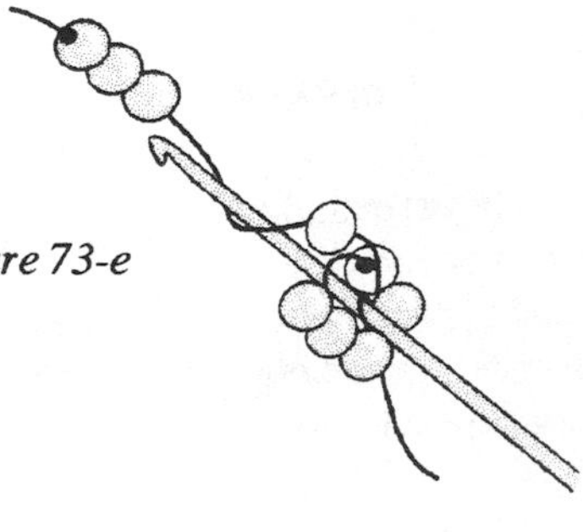

Figure 73-e

Clasp With tail of thread and needle, sew eye pin loop to end of cord jewelry, approximately 3 stitches for strength (*Figure 74*-a). Tie off with a regular sewing knot and work end of thread up center of piece about 1". Exit through beads, cut. Add a dab of clear nail polish on knot to seal. Slip bell cap over end of eye pin and position over beads. With round nose pliers, make a loop close to bell cap (*Figure 74-b*). Cut excess wire with wire cutters. Add jump ring and clasp. Repeat on other end.

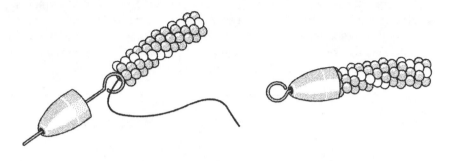

Figures 74-a & 74-b

√ Accurate 4-1 bead count when stringing beads to thread is important for a single stripe crocheted spiral. If a mistake is found after they are all strung-- i.e., 3-1 or 5-1, the error can be broken out instead of restringing.

√ Break a bead by using a pair of small wire cutters. Place the cutter jaws end to end on the bead and squeeze. The bead will break instantly. Be careful not to cut thread.

√ When first learning, use white thread. Black thread is difficult to see, especially when the loop is dropped and disappears into the crochet work.

√ If the crochet loop should slip off the hook, a regular sewing needle works well for retrieving.

√ Check for single beads protruding out of line from the crocheted work before tying off. This is caused by a bead not being looped around properly (*Figure 73-e*) Take out to that point and redo.

Necklace

Follow directions for cord bracelet, just make longer. The necklace can be made entirely of crocheted beaded cord. Another choice is to only make the beaded cord approximately 11 inches long. Then add a pretty sterling silver or gold filled chain between the bell cap and the clasp on both ends, connecting with jump rings on both ends of chain. This gives the necklaces a very expensive look (see color photo insert).

Key Chains

Materials Needed ****

100 DB Beads per inch of cord crocheted
 18 3 mm Gold Filled
  6 2x6 mm Gold S/L Twist Bugle Beads
 12 4 mm S/L Transparent Metallic Iris
  1 2 inch Eye Pin
  1 Bell Cap
  1 24 mm Key Ring (split ring)
Size 13 or 14 Crochet Hook
Size 12 English Needle
2 3/4 yards Black Size D Nymo® Thread

Wire Wrap

Follow instructions for cord bracelet, only crochet a section about 1 1/4" long. Attach an eye pin and bell cap to one end as explained earlier. Instead of just making a loop on the other end of the eye pin as before, wire wrap will be needed for strength. Some key rings may need to be added at this point. Do not cut off excess wire after forming the loop. With one pair of regular needle nose pliers grasping loop firmly, use a second pair to wrap the straight section of wire 2-3 times tightly around the wire section that is between the loop and bell cap (insert). Cut off excess. On the other end, create 5 or 6 loop fringe approximately 2 1/2" long. The thread will have to be repositioned to come directly out of a hole in one the beads along the bottom. Even though there are only 5 beads per row of crochet, there is a half bead showing from the previous row along the bottom allowing for a 6th fringe. Hang DB 27 fringe from the DB 27 beads and the one DB 42 fringe from the single DB 42 bead of crochet work. Tie off with sewing knot in center end of crochet work. Run needle up through center of crochet and out through beads about 1" up, cut. Dab knot with clear nail polish to seal.

DB 27 Metallic Teal Iris
DB 42 S/L Gold

Miscellaneous Beads

3 mm Gold Filled
4 mm S/L Trans. Metallic Iris
2x6 mm S/L Gold Twist Bugle

Daisy Chain

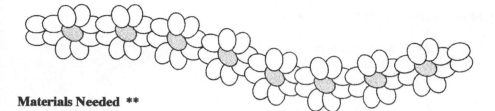

Materials Needed **

11/o Seed Beads (2 contrasting colors)
  2 Double Cup Bead Tips
  2 Jump Rings
  1 Clasp
Size 12 English Needle
3 yds. White Size D Nymo® (Necklace)
1 3/4 yds. White Size D Nymo® (Bracelet)

This is an enjoyable and easy project to make. Depending on the length, it can be a wrist or ankle bracelet, choker, or full-length necklace. DB beads do not work well with this design. They do not form into very nice daisies because of their cylinder shape.

Thread 4 beads on approximately 1 3/4 to 3 yards of thread (increase or decrease thread according to project being made). Position the beads about 8 inches from the end leaving enough to add clasp later. Holding the beads in place with the thumb and forefinger, bring the needle around and go back through the beads in the same direction. Pull the beads side by side (*Figure 76-a*). Pick up six beads of the same color to form daisy petals. Loop around and go through bead shown (*Figure 76-b*). Pull into place.

Pick a contrasting color for the center bead of the daisy and go through bead as shown (*Figure 76-c*), pull into place. Add two more beads (*Figure 76-d*). Repeat (from *Figure 76-b* through *Figure 76-d*) until desired length.

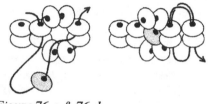

Figure 76-c & 76-d

Attach a double cup bead tip and bead. Go back through the two end beads (*Figure 76-e*). Repeat a second time to give strength. Tie off in body of beads and run the tail of the thread through 5 or more beads before cutting. With needle nose pliers, squeeze the double cups of the bead tip together around the bead. Add jump ring and clasp to the hook part of the bead tip. Close with round nose pliers. Do the same on the other end.

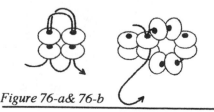

Figure 76-a & 76-b

Figure 76-e

Double Daisy Chain

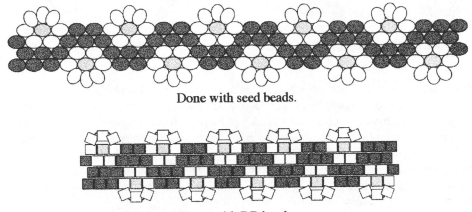

Done with seed beads.

Done with DB beads.

Materials Needed ***

11/o Seed Bead (3 Colors)
Completed Length , 7" with 28 Daisies
- Bronze
- White Pearl
- Clear Yellow

DB Beads (3 Colors)
Completed Length 7" with 34 Daisies
- DB 25 Metallic Blue Iris
- DB 203 Ceylon Yellow
- DB 681 Semi-Matte S/L Squash

2 Double Cup Bead Tips
2 Jump Rings
1 Clasp
Size 12 English Needle
2 1/2 yds. White Size D Nymo® Thread

As you can see, more beads and daisies are required to complete the same length of bracelet using DB beads. The two are made the same but look very different when completed.

The Double Daisy Chain is done with a peyote stitch with beaded loops incorporated along the outer edge to form the outside petals of the daisies.

Add a stop bead about 10 inches from the end of the thread. This will keep the first beads from slipping off and will be removed later. Start with 2 bronze, 2 white pearl and 1 clear yellow. Pass the needle through third bead strung, pull beads into place, adjust. Add a bronze bead, pass the needle through the first bronze bead strung (*Figure 77-a*). Add another bronze bead (*Figure 77-b*). Continue in this fashion with the white and yellow beads (*Figure 78-a* through *Figure 78-c*) on next page.

3rd-

1st-

Figures 77-a & 77-b

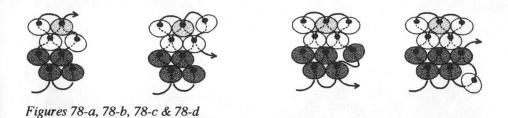

Figures 78-a, 78-b, 78-c & 78-d

At this point, the first white pearl bead of the next flower is added (*Figure 78-d*). Add another bronze bead (*Figure 78-e*). The loop of outer petals of the daisy are added now. Coming out the right side of the daisy, add 3 white pearl beads (*Figure 78-e*), go down the left side of the daisy and loop around coming out the right side, pull down. Continue with a bronze then white pearl bead (*Figure 78-f*), turn work over and add a clear yellow bead (not shown). Repeat (*Figure 76-a* through *Figure 78-f*)) until desired length. Do not add the single white pearl (*Figure 78-d*) when the 34th (or 28th with seed beads) flower is 1/2 complete. Add a bronze bead in it's place.

Finish ends of bracelet as shown in illustration (*Figure 78-g*), adding double cup bead tip with bead between the two bronze beads at the end, looping around as shown starting at solid arrow. Repeat for added strength. Weave end of thread in securely, cut. Add jump ring and clasp. Finish other end in same manner.

This design makes a better wrist bracelet than necklace or ankle bracelet. They do not contour very well to the neck or ankle.

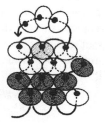 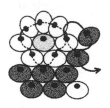 

Figures 78-e, 78-f & 78-g

Glossary of Terms

AB Aurora Borealis, a finish on transparent beads and crystals that gives a rainbow effect.

Bead Cap Used to cover and finish off end of work. The eye pin is run through the hole at the top, a loop is made, the jump ring and clasp are attached.

Ceylon Pearl-like finish on opaque beads.

Double Cup Bead Tip Used to conceal knots at the ends of bead work and to connect to clasp.

Eye Pin Looks like a thick straight pin with a loop on one end. It is used to interconnect the end of a work with jump ring and clasp.

Finding Clasps, jump rings, ear wires, head pins and other parts needed to finish or assemble earrings, bracelets, necklaces, pins, etc.

Hank Seed beads are usually sold in hanks. The packages consist of 12 individual strands of the same bead, each strand is about 12 inches long, all tied together at the top.

Head Pin Looks like an over-sized straight pin. Used for beaded dangles.

Iris A finish on opaque beads to give a purple rainbow effect.

Gram There are 28 grams to 1 ounce.

Jump Rings A small metal ring that joins things. To open, hold with two pairs of pliers, one on each side of the opening. Spread the opening sideways, not apart. This allows it to be re-closed without leaving a gap.

Kilo 100 grams

Luster Clear coating on beads that give a high gloss.

Matte Dull frosted appearance.

Metallic An opaque coating over a bead. Colors such as gold, copper, silver. Many of these coating will eventually rub off. Clear nail polish can help prolong life.

Opaque Solid, not transparent.

Stop Bead A single bead tied in place about 8-10 inches from end of thread. Used to temporarily hold first beads in place on thread until enough beads are woven to hold everything together. Knot, or sometimes bead, is removed when beads are stable.

Other Titles Offered

Beaded Images, *Intricate Beaded Jewelry Using Brick Stitch* - by Barbara Elbe
Contains: Sculptured parrots, peacocks and many vertical patterns. A chance
to break away from the traditional brick stitch earring mold. Also sculptured
Santa earrings, snowmen, candy canes and 3- dimensional wreaths, Christmas
trees and reindeer pins. A total of 33 unique patterns using Delica and Hexagon
beads. Size 14/o seed beads can be substituted. 4 color plates, 80 pages.

Beaded Images II, *Intricate Beaded Jewelry Using Brick Stitch* - by Barbara Elbe
Contains: Sculptured earring designs using horizontal and vertical base rows.
Including: Horses, penguins, cats and flying mallard ducks. There are girls
and clowns with three-dimensional curly hair. Bead sculpturing is fully
explained (increasing and decreasing the number of beads in a row) with 29
patterns in all using Delica beads. 4 color plates, 72 pages.

Order Form

Beaded Images   -   by Barbara Elbe   _____   x $ 9.95 = _____
Beaded Images II   -   by Barbara Elbe   _____   x $ 9.95 = _____
Back to Beadin'   -   by Barbara E. Elbe   _____   x $11.95 = _____

CA Residents 7.25% Sales Tax   _____

Shipping: $2.00 for first book
$ .75 for each additional book   _____

TOTAL ENCLOSED   _____

Check or Money Order Payable to: Barbara Elbe
                                        556 Hanland Court
                                        Redding, CA 96003
                                        (916) 244-0317

Name_____

Address _____

City/State/Zip _____

Phone_____